Collected Poems

THE MACMILLAN COMPANY
NEW YORK · CHICAGO
DALLAS · ATLANTA · SAN FRANCISCO

THE MACMILLAN COMPANY
OF CANADA, LIMITED
TORONTO

JAMES STEPHENS

Collected Poems

NEW, REVISED AND ENLARGED EDITION

NEW YORK   THE MACMILLAN COMPANY   1954

First Printing

GEORGE W. RUSSELL (A.E.)

with homage and
affection

Preface

A CHRONOLOGICAL order in the printing of verse is useful as showing the growth of technique, and perhaps also in demonstrating the maturing of emotion and thought in a writer: but the lack of sequence in mood and subject consequent on such a method can be distressing to the reader. I have thought best, therefore, to arrange these poems in subject-sequence, as indicated by the sub-titles to the sections into which this book is divided.

I have discarded a great number of poems for the very best of reasons, but I have retained some that were lately almost universally condemned; for example, the twenty-six-word arpeggio beginning "He wills to be alone with thee" and a tiny balancing measure entitled, "The Main-Deep."

It is said that this is the day of the lyric, and the fact that it has been said indicates some displeasure on the part of those who made the discovery. A considerable part of our discoveries are only brought into consciousness by reason of the annoyance which they first, unconsciously, visited upon us. When we examine the sense of exasperation and thwarting that is expressed on the subject of literature it is well to recollect that every other art is evolving in the same way, and is evoking the same distress among its adepts and votaries.

The world-interest to-day differs notably from that which gave it enthusiasm and stability in the past, for, within the last thirty years, the tempo of the whole world has been enormously accelerated. It is still accelerating, and the technique that we inherited, in whatever art, from a leisured society is not equal to the demands that are now made upon it, and which demands are still incoherent if not unconscious. We must evolve a new technique, or we must continue to compose and paint and write in the only form that can deal with an interim situation, or with speed—the lyrical form.

A revival of epic is not to be wished; nor, while the general mind is steeped in what is practically a new element, is such a revival possible. Epic will only deal with matured, with thoroughly absorbed, mental or spiritual cognitions. It comes at the end of an era, and is a summary, or a reduction to mythological form, of all that its era meant. We are at the beginning of an era, and who creates a new world must create a new art to express it. Already a large proportion of the writings that we call classical have lost their authority, and that not by being outmoded. It is not time but change that is consigning these to oblivion. Another mind than that they reckoned with is consigning them to oblivion, and thumbs may be turned down to all that could interest and excite the élite of only a generation ago.

It is almost terrifying to consider upon how slight a basis of agreement and tact are founded all our ideas of art or philosophy or even religion, and how small a universal change could transform these out of all recognition. The change that man makes without him is summed in the mind, and must at some time recognise itself. But occultations of whatever nature are not to be over-mourned. The earth is not the poorer for the lost leaves of yesteryear; nor, whatever he seems to lose, will man really suffer a deprivation. The earth and he—what they have they hold, and all their phases are normal.

Having been discovered, lyric, like everything else that is thus "found out", must fall into disrepute, and may indeed join the arts that were lost before it—epic, tragedy, romance, gaiety: lost arts all! And, for a time, until a norm of experience is re-established, prose must do the world's work, and we may, perhaps confidently, expect a prose renaissance.

Here there is cause for speculation. We cannot foresee the means whereby prose can renew itself. Nothing that is outworn or over-borne can salve itself by its own virtue, for, were that virtue capable, it had not been overborne. It may only be retrieved by the assault of a competitive antagonist. The transcription of action for the sake of action lies upon all prose like a veritable disease. As a subject, action can achieve a really amazing cleverness; and it is probable that the prose-writing of the world has never been so clever or so various as it is to-day. But, also, prose-writing has never been so mentally lazy as it is to-day, and the lack of fundamental brain-work, so evident in our novelists and essayists, is not compensated for by their as evident agility. By taking over the story of action the cinema will force prose to reconsider its means, and to discover its special or latent aptitudes. This taking-over seems inevitable.

A whole series of modes belong to lyrical poetry: they compose the infinity which art requires, and within which the lyrical poet may consider that there is nothing whatever which he cannot do. Lacking the feeling of power which this infinity provides, an artist is helpless. It may be said that the lyrical poet is undisputed master of all the *extremes* that can be expressed in terms of time or speed or tempo. No pen but his can hold excessive velocity or excessive slowness. A swift lyrical line is as quick as lightning; a slow one can be slower than a snail; and it is only in these difficult regions, distant regions, that the poet can work with ease and certainty.

All normal speeds are properly in the care of the prose-writer, and it might be held that the greatest glory of a prose-writer is to be pedestrian. His problems, technically, are more numerous and more difficult than are those that engage his lyrical and epical brethren. The matter under description is, for the prose-writer, a complete interest. He cannot depart from it; nor treat it disrespectfully; nor overlook any of its parts. To observe his matter, to analyse it, and, if he can, to ornament it, is his whole duty. Like the scientist, he can refuse to be interested in God, or in any abstract matter whatever, on condition that he is thoroughly interested in matter and its modes. And, in this sphere, the perfection that he can arrive at, or aim at, is as splendid as is that of any other artist.

The poet needs not to observe or analyse in the sense that a prose-writer must, for his business does not lie with details or parts. He will apprehend and generalise. His apparent matter is not of final consequence; it needs not even to be of intrinsic interest, and it may be no more for him than a ground of departure and arrival. That which he adds to the formal matter is not liable to definition although it is obvious and an object of knowledge. Nor is poetry amenable to criticism in the sense that prose is—for prose can be criticised even when it is good, but only bad poetry (if there be such a thing) can be halted for examination. It may be said that the poet energises matter more highly than prose can manage, and that it is this excess of energy which we recognise as poetry. The duty of a lyrical poet is not to express or explain, it is to intensify life, and its essence is properly indefinable.

The epic poet differs in both technique and content from these other artists; and, as used by him, the blank-verse form is incomparably the subtlest, the greatest instrument that literary art has evolved. The matter that can be submitted to this form must be the gravest that the mind can conceive, and, naturally, the most intensely comprehended. It must also be a matter that can be held, as it were, stationary. All speeds are at rest in this form. We may not ask at what pace it moves, nor require any movement whatever from it. It is always deeply religious. It is always romantic or truth-telling. Nothing, in human terms, has been finally uttered until it has been said in blank-verse, or its equivalent in whatever language.

A lyrical movement in prose is a disfiguring intruder in that art. A lyrical interruption in blank-verse is just as unhappy. In either event, the additional matter fashions a relief that is unpleasant because it is unnecessary: imposing, in the one case, a pace that makes prose seem under-vitalised, and adding, in the other, an activity that cannot but appear trivial.

There is an affinity between blank-verse and prose. As an aristocrat may, without loss of dignity, take on certain aspects of his peasantry, so blank-verse (or epic) can neighbour prose if it wishes to do so. But, in either of these cases, the converse cannot happen. The peasant can, indeed, learn something of fine or subtil manners from his aristocratic contemporary, and the prose-writer can learn the same if he will humbly, that is, affectionately, study epic. If workers in prose did this they could almost afford to study nothing else.

JAMES STEPHENS

Contents

BOOK II

A HONEYCOMB

BOOK III

IN THE TWO LIGHTS

BOOK IV

HEELS AND HEAD

BOOK V

LESS THAN DAINTILY

BOOK VI

THE GOLDEN BIRD

BOOK VII

STRICT JOY

BOOK VIII

KINGS AND THE MOON

BOOK IX

ADDITIONAL

Book I

IN GREEN WAYS

The Goat Paths

THE crooked paths
Go every way
Upon the hill
—They wind about
Through the heather,
In and out
Of a quiet
Sunniness.

And the goats,
Day after day,
Stray
In sunny
Quietness;
Cropping here,
And cropping there
—As they pause,
And turn,
And pass—
Now a bit
Of heather spray,
Now a mouthful
Of the grass.

2

In the deeper
Sunniness;
In the place
Where nothing stirs;
Quietly
In quietness;
In the quiet
Of the furze
They stand a while;
They dream;
They lie;
They stare
Upon the roving sky.

If you approach
They run away!
They will stare,
And stamp,
And bound,
With a sudden angry sound,
To the sunny
Quietude;
To crouch again,
Where nothing stirs,
In the quiet
Of the furze:
To crouch them down again,
And brood,
In the sunny
Solitude.

3

Were I but
As free

As they,
I would stray
Away
And brood;
I would beat
A hidden way,
Through the quiet
Heather spray,
To a sunny
Solitude.

And should you come
I'd run away!
I would make an angry sound,
I would stare,
And stamp,
And bound
To the deeper
Quietude;
To the place
Where nothing stirs
In the quiet
Of the furze.

4

In that airy
Quietness
I would dream
As long as they:
Through the quiet
Sunniness
I would stray
Away
And brood,
All among

The heather spray,
In a sunny
Solitude.

—I would think
Until I found
Something
I can never find;
—Something
Lying
On the ground,
In the bottom
Of my mind.

The Fifteen Acres

I CLING and swing
On a branch, or sing
Through the cool clear hush of morning O!

Or fling my wing
On the air, and bring
To sleepier birds a warning O!

That the night's in flight!
And the sun's in sight!
And the dew is the grass adorning O!

And the green leaves swing
As I sing, sing, sing:
Up by the river,
Down the dell,
To the little wee nest,
Where the big tree fell,
So early in the morning O!

II

I flit and twit
In the sun for a bit,
When his light so bright is shining O!

7

Or sit, and fit
My plumes, or knit
Straw plaits for the nest's nice lining O!

And she, with glee,
Shows unto me,
Underneath her wing reclining O!

And I sing that Peg
Has an egg, egg, egg!
Up by the oat-field,
Round the mill;
Past the meadow,
Down the hill;
So early in the morning O!

III

I stoop and swoop
On the air, or loop
Through the trees, and then go soaring O!

To group, with a troop,
On the skiey poop,
While the wind behind is roaring O!

I skim and swim
By a cloud's red rim;
And up to the azure flooring O!

And my wide wings drip,
As I slip, slip, slip,
Down through the rain-drops,
Back where Peg
Broods in the nest
On the little white egg,
So early in the morning O!

The Rivals

I HEARD a bird at dawn
Singing sweetly on a tree,
That the dew was on the lawn,
And the wind was on the lea;
But I didn't listen to him,
For he didn't sing to me!

I didn't listen to him,
For he didn't sing to me
That the dew was on the lawn,
And the wind was on the lea!
I was singing at the time,
Just as prettily as he!

I was singing all the time,
Just as prettily as he,
About the dew upon the lawn,
And the wind upon the lea!
So I didn't listen to him,
As he sang upon a tree!

Follow, Follow, Follow

FOLLOW! Follow! Follow!
Blackbird, thrush and swallow!
The air is soft, the sun is dancing through
The dancing boughs;
A little while me company along
And I will go with you.
Arouse! Arouse!
Among the leaves I sing my pleasant song.

Sky! Sky! On high! O gentle majesty!
Come all ye happy birds and follow, follow!
Under the slender interlacing boughs,
Blackbird, thrush and swallow!
No longer in the sunlight sit and drowse
But me accompany along;
No longer be ye mute!
Arouse! Arouse!
Among the leaves I sing my pleasant song.

Lift, lift, ye happy birds! Lift song and wing;
And sing and fly; and fly again, and sing
Up to the very blueness of the sky
Your happy words!
O Follow! Follow! Follow!

Where we go racing through the shady ways,
Blackbird, thrush and swallow,
Shouting aloud our ecstasy of praise!
Under the slender interlacing boughs
Me company along;
The sun is coming with us!
Rouse! O rouse!
Among the leaves I sing my pleasant song.

Minuette

I

THE moon shines,
And the wind blows,
And the heart knows,

Carelessly, and carelessly!
That to them each thing inclines,
And that everything is free!

All that is, is given to thee!
Take the love, that comes and goes!
Uncomplaining, thankless, be,

As the moon, the bird, the rose,
Thankless, uncomplaining, are
Beauty, Music, and a Star!

II

Call, and come, and come, and call!
Nothing is denied the gay!
All to each, and each to all.

Fall, and flow, and go away;
As the moon shines, and the heart knows;
Carelessly, as the wind blows!

Not for duty we fulfil
Lovely motions—'tis for naught!
All the will of good and ill,

All of ignorance, and thought,
All are harmless, if we are
Free as Wind, and Rose, and Star.

III

Taking all of cherishing
That befall, or may not fall,
As a happy, chancing, thing,

Some for each, and all for all;
Taking all the haps that be,
Carelessly, and carelessly!

Life comes on, with not a word;
Love is love, on no demand;
Death, unasked, hath him bestirred,

Lifting all up by the hand:
All that fall he stoops above
Lovingly, for he is Love!

IV

Love is round, and round, and round!
Everywhere, in every spot,
It is lost, and it is found,

Here it is—and here is not!
Man, and beast, and bird, and snake,
Take, and take, and take, and take,

As the Moon takes up the sight!
As the Rose takes up the shower!
As the Heart takes all Delight,

Might and Beauty for its dower!
All that is—for all is free—
Take carelessly, and carelessly!

And It Was Windy Weather

Now the winds are riding by;
Clouds are galloping the sky;

Bush and tree are lashing bare,
Savage, boughs on savage air;

Crying, as they lash and sway,
—Pull the roots out of the clay!

Lift away: away:
Away!

Leave security, and speed
From the root, the mud, the mead!

Into sea and air, we go!
To chase the gull, the moon!—and know

—Flying high!
Flying high!—

All the freedom of the sky!
All the freedom of the sky!

Dance

I

Left and right and swing around!
Soar and dip and fall for glee!
Happy sky, and bird, and ground!
Happy wind, and happy tree!

Happy minions, dancing mad!
Joy is guide enough for you;
Cure the world of good and bad;
And teach us innocence anew!

2

Good and bad and right and wrong!
Wave the silly words away!
This is wisdom—to be strong!
This is virtue—to be gay!

Let us sing and dance, until
We shall know the final art;
How to banish good and ill
With the laughter of the heart!

The Centaurs

PLAYING upon the hill three centaurs were!
They lifted each a hoof! They stared at me!
And stamped the dust!

They stamped the dust! They snuffed upon the air!
And all their movements had the fierce glee
Of power, and pride, and lust!

Of power and pride and lust! Then, with a shout,
They tossed their heads, and wheeled, and galloped round,
In furious brotherhood!

In furious brotherhood! Around, about,
They charged, they swerved, they leaped! Then, bound on bound,
They raced into the wood!

The Crackling Twig

THERE came a satyr creeping through the wood,
His hair fell on his breast, his legs were slim:
His eyes were dancing wickedly, he stood,
He peeped about on every side of him.

He danced! He peeped! But, at a sound I made,
A crackling twig, he turned; and, suddenly,
In three great jumps, he bounded to the shade,
And disappeared among the greenery!

In the Night

THERE always is a noise when it is dark!
It is the noise of silence, and the noise
Of blindness!

The noise of silence, and the noise of blindness
Do frighten me!
They hold me stark and rigid as a tree!

These frighten me!
These hold me stark and rigid as a tree!
Because at last their tumult is more loud
Than thunder!

Because at last
Their tumult is more loud than thunder,
They terrify my soul! They tear
My heart asunder!

The Lark

THERE is a small bird cowering in the dark;
His wing is broken, he will no more sing;
He will not fly, nor sing again, the lark
With a broken wing!

The bird that cowers with a broken wing
Is all alone—His mate has gone away:
In the morrow, in the sun, in the field, his mate will sing
Her wonted lay.

In the dew, in the limpid dawn, in the ray
Of the sun, she'll sing the comrade gone
Who will not cheer a sunny day
Again for any one.

.   .   .

All panic looks and listens with his eyes!
He is all fear! He is no more a lark!
Only the heart dares stir of him that lies
In the dark!

The Snare

I HEAR a sudden cry of pain!
There is a rabbit in a snare:
Now I hear the cry again,
But I cannot tell from where.

But I cannot tell from where
He is calling out for aid!
Crying on the frightened air,
Making everything afraid!

Making everything afraid!
Wrinkling up his little face!
As he cries again for aid;
—And I cannot find the place!

And I cannot find the place
Where his paw is in the snare!
Little One! Oh, Little One!
I am searching everywhere!

Little Things

Little things, that run, and quail,
And die, in silence and despair!

Little things, that fight, and fail,
And fall, on sea, and earth, and air!

All trapped and frightened little things,
The mouse, the coney, hear our prayer!

As we forgive those done to us,
—The lamb, the linnet, and the hare—

Forgive us all our trespasses,
Little creatures, everywhere!

Lovers

THE moon is shining on the sea!
Every night the moon looks down
Through the spaces, quietly:
And, no matter though I be
Among the houses of the town,
Something always says to me,
—The moon is shining on the sea—!

Along the boulevard I pace,
Looking for her through the trees,
And I see her gentle face
Beaming through immensities:
And, as I look, there comes to me
The lonely murmur of the sea.

All across all that is space
They are telling their distress;
They are looking, face to face,
All longing, and all loneliness;
The pretty, timid moon, and the
Poor, unhappy, little sea.

Chill of the Eve

A LONG green swell
Slopes soft to the sea;
And a far-off bell
Swings sweet to me;
As the grey
Chill day
Slips away
From the lea.

Spread cold and far,
Without one glow
From a mild pale star,
Is the sky's steel bow;
And the grey
Chill day
Slips away
Below.

Yon green tree grieves
To the air around;
And the whispering leaves
Have a lonely sound;
As the grey
Chill day

Slips away
From the ground.

And dark, more dark,
The shades settle down;
Far off is a spark
From the lamp-lit town;
And the grey
Chill day
Slips away
With a frown.

The Shell

AND then I pressed the shell
Close to my ear,
And listened well.

And straightway, like a bell,
Came low and clear
The slow, sad, murmur of far distant seas

Whipped by an icy breeze
Upon a shore
Wind-swept and desolate.

It was a sunless strand that never bore
The footprint of a man.
Nor felt the weight

Since time began
Of any human quality or stir,
Save what the dreary winds and wave incur.

And in the hush of waters was the sound
Of pebbles, rolling round;
For ever rolling, with a hollow sound:

And bubbling sea-weeds, as the waters go,
Swish to and fro
Their long cold tentacles of slimy grey:

There was no day;
Nor ever came a night
Setting the stars alight

To wonder at the moon:
Was twilight only, and the frightened croon,
Smitten to whimpers, of the dreary wind

And waves that journeyed blind . . .
And then I loosed my ear—Oh, it was sweet
To hear a cart go jolting down the street.

The Main-Deep

THE long-rólling,
Steady-póuring,
Deep-trenchéd
Green billów:

The wide-topped,
Unbróken,
Green-glacid,
Slow-sliding,

Cold-flushing,
—On—on—on—
Chill-rushing,
Hush—hushing,

. . . Hush—hushing . . .

The County Mayo

Now, with the coming in of the spring, the days will stretch a bit;
And after the Feast of Brigid I shall hoist my flag and go:
For, since the thought got into my head, I can neither stand nor sit
Until I find myself in the middle of the County of Mayo.

In Claremorris I should stop a night to sleep with decent men;
And then I'd go to Balla, just beyond, and drink galore;
And next I'd stay in Kiltimagh for about a month; and then
I should only be a couple of miles away from Ballymore!

I say and swear that my heart lifts up like the lifting of a tide;
Rising up like the rising wind till fog or mist must go,
When I remember Carra, and Gallen close beside,
And the Gap of the Two Bushes, and the wide plains of Mayo.

To Killaden then, to the place where everything grows that is best;
There are raspberries there, and strawberries there, and all that is good
    for men;
And were I only there, among my folk, my heart would rest,
For age itself would leave me there, and I'd be young again.

Spring
1916

I

Do not forget my charge, I beg of you;
That of what flowers you find, of fairest hue
And sweetest odour, you do gather those
Are best of all the best—

A fragrant rose;
A tall calm lily from the waterside;
A half-blown poppy hanging at the side
Its head of dream,
Dreaming among the corn:
Forget-me-nots, that seem
As though the morn
Had tumbled down, and grew into the clay;
And buds that sway,
And swing along the way,
Easing the hearts of those who pass them by
Until they find contentment—

Do not cry!
But gather buds! And, with them, greenery
Of slender branches taken from a tree
Well bannered by the Spring that saw them fall:

And you, for you are cleverest of all,
Who have slim fingers and are pitiful!
Brimming your lap with bloom that you may cull,
Will sit apart, and weave for every head
A garland of the flowers you gatheréd.

II

Be green upon their graves, O happy Spring!
For they were young and eager who are dead!
Of all things that are young, and quivering
With eager life, be they rememberéd!
They move not here! They have gone to the clay!
They cannot die again for liberty!
Be they remembered of their land for aye!
Green be their graves, and green their memory!

Fragrance and beauty come in with the green!
The ragged bushes put on sweet attire!
The birds forget how chill these airs have been!
The clouds bloom out again in limpid fire!
Blue dawns the day! Blue calm lies on the lake,
And merry sounds are fitful in the thorn!
In covert green the young blackbirds awake;
They shake their wings, and sing upon the morn.

At springing of the year you came and swung
Green flags above the newly-greening earth;
Scarce were the leaves unfolded, they were young,
Nor had outgrown the wrinkles of their birth:
Comrades they thought you of their pleasant hour,
Who had but glimpsed the sun when they saw you!
Who heard your song ere birds had singing power,
And drank your blood or e'er they drank the dew.

Then you went down! And then, and as in pain,
The Spring, affrighted, fled her leafy ways!

The clouds came to the earth in gusty rain!
And no sun shone again for many days!
And day by day they told that one was dead!
And day by day the season mourned for you!
Until that count of woe was finishéd,
And Spring remembered all was yet to do!

She came with mirth of wind and eager leaf;
With scampering feet and reaching out of wings;
She laughed among the boughs and banished grief,
And cared again for all her baby things:
Leading along the joy that has to be!
Bidding her timid buds think on the May!
And told, that Summer comes—with victory!
And told the hope that is all creatures' stay.

Go, Winter, now unto your own abode,
Your time is done, and Spring is conqueror!
Lift up with all your gear and take your road!
For she is here, and brings the sun with her!
Now are we born again, and now are we,
—Wintered so long beneath an icy hand!—
New-risen into life and liberty,
Because the Spring is come into our land!

III

In other lands they may,
With public joy or dole along the way,
With pomp and pageantry and loud lament

Of drums and trumpets; or with merriment
Of grateful hearts, lead into rest and stead
The nation's dead.

If we had drums and trumpets! If we had
Aught of heroic pitch, or accent glad,
To honour you—as bids tradition old—

With banners flung, or draped in mournful fold,
And pacing cortège! These should we not bring
For your last journeying!

We have no drums or trumpets! Naught have we,
But some green branches taken from a tree,
And flowers that grow at large in mead and vale!

Nothing of choice have we! Nor of avail
To do you honour, as our honour deems,
And as your worth beseems!

Wait, drums and trumpets, yet a little time!
All ends, and all begins! And there is chime
At last where discord was! And joy, at last,

Where woe wept out her eyes! Be not downcast!
Here is prosperity and goodly cheer,
For life does follow death! And death is here!

IV

Joy be with us, and honour close the tale!
Now do we dip the prow, and shake the sail,
And take the wind, and bid adieu to rest!

With gladness now we re-begin the quest
That destiny commands! Though where we go
Or guided by what star, no man doth know!

Uncharted is our course! Our hearts untried!
And we may weary ere we take the tide,
Or make fair haven from the moaning sea.

Be ye propitious, winds of destiny!
On us at first blow not too boisterous bold!
All Ireland hath is packed into this hold!

Her hopes fly at the peak! Now it is dawn
And we away—Be with us, Mananán!

Song, I Am Tired to Death

SONG! I am tired to death! Here let me lie
Where we have placed the moving trees along!
Till I recover from my ecstasy,
Farewell, my Song!

Once more unto your pipe I lend my rhyme,
Who went in woodland ways with you along!
We have been happy for a little time!
Farewell, my Song!

Soon, soon, return, or all my life is naught!
Come soon, and we will pace the woods along;
And tell unto each other all our thought!
Farewell, my Song!

And when, again, you do come back to me,
Under the sounding trees we'll pace along:
While to your pipe I raise my poesy:
Farewell, my Song!

Book II

A HONEYCOMB

To the Queen of the Bees

BEE! tell me, whence do you come?
Ten fields away, twenty perhaps,
Have heard your hum.

If you are from the north, you may
Have passed my mother's roof of straw
Upon your way.

If you come from the south, you should
Have seen a little cottage just
Inside a wood.

And should you go back that way, please
Carry a message to the house
Among the trees.

Say—I shall meet her at the rock
Beside the stream, this very night
At eight o'clock.

And ask your queen, when you get home,
To send my queen the present of
A honeycomb.

Lesbia

SWEET,
And delicate,
And rare,

At the end
Of a wind-blown fragrant bough,
The apple swings!

If I,
Who fly no more,
Had wings!

Or if
My wizardry
Knew how!

I'd wing
To where that sweetness swings,
—At the end of the bough!

Mary Hynes

1

SHE is the sky
Of the sun!
She is the dart
Of love!

She is the love
Of my heart!
She is a rune!
She is above

The women
Of the race of Eve
As the sun
Is above the moon!

2

Lovely and airy
The view from the hill
That looks down
Ballylea!

But no good sight
Is good, until

By great good luck
You see

The Blossom
Of the Branches,
Walking towards you,
Airily!

The Wood of Flowers

I WENT to the Wood of Flowers,
No one went with me;
I was there alone for hours;
I was happy as could be,
In the Wood of Flowers!

There was grass
On the ground;
There were leaves
On the tree;

And the wind
Had a sound
Of such sheer
Gaiety,

That I
Was as happy
As happy could be,
In the Wood of Flowers!

Peggy Mitchell

As lily grows up easily,
In modest, gentle dignity,
To sweet perfection,
—So grew she,
As easily!

Or as the rose,
That takes no care,
Will open out, on sunny air,
Bloom after bloom,
Fair after fair;
Just so did she
—As carelessly!

She is our torment without end!
She is our enemy, our friend!
Our joy, our woe!
And she will send
Madness, or glee,
To you, or me,
—And endlessly!

Sweet Apple

At the end of the bough!
At the top of the tree!
—As fragrant, as high,
And as lovely, as thou—
One sweet apple reddens,
Which all men may see,
—At the end of the bough!

Swinging full to the view!
Though the harvesters now
Overlook it, repass it,
And pass busily:
Overlook it!
Nay, pluck it!
They do not know how!

For it swings out of reach
Like a cloud! And as free
As a star; or thy beauty,
That seems too, I vow,
Remote as the sweet apple, swinging
—Ah me!
At the end of the bough!

The Canal Bank

I KNOW a girl,
And a girl knows me,
And the owl says, what!
And the owl says, who?

But what we know
We both agree
That nobody else
Shall hear or see;

It's all between herself and me:
To wit? said the owl,
To woo! said I,
To-what! To-wit! To-woo!

The Coolin

COME with me, under my coat,
And we will drink our fill
Of the milk of the white goat,
Or wine if it be thy will.

And we will talk, until
Talk is a trouble, too,
Out on the side of the hill;
And nothing is left to do,

But an eye to look into an eye;
And a hand in a hand to slip;
And a sigh to answer a sigh;
And a lip to find out a lip!

What if the night be black!
Or the air on the mountain chill!
Where the goat lies down in her track,
And all but the fern is still!

Stay with me, under my coat!
And we will drink our fill
Of the milk of the white goat,
Out on the side of the hill!

Nancy Walsh

It is not on her gown
She fears to tread;
But on her hair
That tumbles down
And strays
About her ways.

And she lives nigh this place!
The dead would rise
Only to see her face!
The dead would rise
Only to hear her sing!

We would leave behind
Both wife and child,
And house and home;
And wander blind,
And wander thus,
And ever roam,
If she would come to us
In Erris.

Softly she said to me
—Be patient till the night comes,
And I will go with thee.

The Daisies

In the scented bud of the morning-O,
When the windy grass went rippling far!
I saw my dear one walking slow
In the field where the daisies are.

We did not laugh, and we did not speak,
As we wandered happily, to and fro;
I kissed my dear on either cheek,
In the bud of the morning-O!

A lark sang up, from the breezy land;
A lark sang down, from a cloud afar;
As she and I went, hand in hand,
In the field where the daisies are.

In Woods and Meadows

PLAY to the tender stops, though cheerily!
Gently my soul, my song! Let no one hear!
Sing to thyself alone! Thine ecstasy
Rising in silence to the inward ear
That is attuned to silence! Do not tell
A friend, a bird, a star, lest they should say

—He danced in woods and meadows all the day,
Waving his arms; and cried, as evening fell,
"O, do not come!"
And cried, "O, come, thou queen!
And walk with me unwatched upon the green
Under the sky!"

The Red Man's Wife

AFTER great fire
Great frost
Comes following!

Turgesius was lost
By the daughter of Maelscheachlin,
The King!

By Grainne,
Of high Ben Gulbain in the north,
Was Diarmuid lost!

The strong sons of Uisneac,
Who never submitted,
They fell by Deirdre!

49

The Buds

Now I can see
The buds are green again
On every tree.

Through the dear intercourse of sun and dew,
Of thrilling root, and folding earth, anew
They come, in beauty.

They up to the sun,
As on a breast, are lifting every one
Green leaves.

Under the eaves
The sparrows and the swallows
Are in love.

There is a chatter in the woods above,
Where the grim crow
Is telling what his sweetheart wants to know.

For the sun
Is shining fair,
And the green
Is on the tree;

And the wind
Is everywhere
Whispering
So urgently!

You will die
Unless you do
Find a mate
To whisper to.

Nancy Walsh

I, WITHOUT bite or sup,
If thou wert fated for me,
I would up
And would go after thee
Through mountains!

A thousand thanks from me
To God have gone,
Because I did not lose my senses to thee,
Though it was hardly I escaped from thee,
O Ringleted One!

Geoffrey Keating

O WOMAN full of wiliness!
Although for love of me you pine,
Withhold your hand adventurous,
It holdeth nothing, holding mine.

Look on my head, how it is grey!
My body's weakness doth appear;
My blood is chill and thin; my day
Is done, and there is nothing here.

Do not call me a foolish man,
Nor lean your lovely cheek to mine:
O slender witch, our bodies can
Not mingle now, nor any time.

Then take your mouth from mine, your hand
From mine, ah, take those lips away!
Lest thought should ripe to willing, and
All this be grave that had been gay.

It is this curl, a silken nest,
And this grey eye, bright as the dew,
And this round, lovely, snow-white breast
That draws desire in search of you.

I would do all for you, meseems,
But this, tho' this were happiness!
I shall not mingle in your dreams,
O woman full of wiliness!

Green Weeds

To be not jealous, give not love!
Rate not thy fair all fair above,
Or thou'lt be decked in green, the hue
That jealousy is bounden to.

That lily hand! Those lips of fire!
Those dewy eyes that spill desire!
Those mounds of lambent snow, may be
Found anywhere it pleaseth thee

To turn! Then turn, and be not mad
Though all of loveliness she had:
—She hath not *all* of loveliness!
A store remains, wherewith to bless

The bee, the bird, the butterfly,
And thou! Go, search with those that fly
For that, which thou shalt easy find
On every path, and any wind!

Nor dream that she be Seal and Star
Who is but as her sisters are!
And whose reply is, Yes and No,
To all that come, and all that go.

—I love!—Then love again, my friend;
Enjoy thy love, without an end!—
—I love . . . Ah, cease! Know what is what,
Thou dost not love, if she love not!

For if thou truly lovéd her
From thee away she could not stir!
But ever at thy side, would be
Thy self, and thy felicity!

Go! Drape thee in the greeny hue!
Thou art not Love! She is not True!
And, no more need be said—Adieu!

The End of the Road

THIS is a thing is true,
Everything comes to an end!
The loving of me and you,
The walking of friend and friend!

Shall I weep the greatness I knew!
Or the beauty, gathered away!
Or the truth that is only true
—As the things that a man will say?

The child and the mother will die!
The wife and husband sever!
The sun will go out of the sky!
And the rain will be falling for ever!

For ever! Until the waves rear
To the skies, with a terrible tune!
And cover the earth and the air!
And wash up the beach of the moon!

Then go, for all things must end!
And this is true, as I say—
A friend will be leaving a friend!
And a man will be going away!

Mary Ruane

THE sky-like girl that we knew!
She dressed herself to go to the fair
In a dress of white and blue;

A white lace cap, and ribbons white
She wore in her hair;
She does not hear in the night

Her mother crying for her, where
Down, deep, in the sea,
She rolls, and lingers, to and fro,

Unweariedly!

The Watcher

A ROSE for a young head,
A ring for a bride,
Joy for the homestead
Clean and wide
—Who's that waiting
In the rain outside?

A heart for an old friend,
A hand for the new:
Love can to earth lend
Heaven's hue—
—Who's that standing
In the silver dew?

A smile for the parting,
A tear as they go,
God's sweethearting
Ends just so—
—Who's that watching
Where the black winds blow?

He who is waiting
In the rain outside,
He who is standing
Where the dew drops wide,

He who is watching
In the wind must ride

—Tho' the pale hands cling—
With the rose, and the ring,
And the bride;
Must ride,
With the red of the rose,
And the gold of the ring,
And the lips and the hair of the bride.

To the Tree

BALLAD! I have a message you must bear
Unto a certain tree! I may not tell
Where she abides; only, she is more fair
Than any tree that grows down in a dell;
Or on a mountain top; or by a well;
Or as a lovely sentinel beside
A brimming stream! No words can speak her well;
Nor lyric sing enough her arms so wide;
Her grace, her peace, her innocence, her happy pride!

Come, Ballad, quickly back to me again,
After you have delivered to the tree
My humble service; and if she will deign
To trust you with a message back, then see,
Most strictly, you forget no word that she
May speak to you! No smallest yes or no!
And what she looked like when she spoke of me!
And if she begged you stay or bade you go!
Or hesitated, ere she said—what you shall know!

Say—I shall visit her ere day be done;
When the flushed evening blanches to the dark;
When one last ray of all that was the sun
Rests on her topmost branches! When the lark

Dips to the dew-drenched grasses in the park,
And sends but rare from dusky fields below
A sleepy song! Then, swift as to the mark
An arrow flies, so swiftly will I go,
Nor stay until her branches wide I halt below.

Of every tree most beautiful and queen!
The blossom of the wood lives in her glee!
About her feet the forest folk are seen!
The timid nymph bends there a ready knee!
And Pan himself, morose, unwillingly,
Yet all perforce, must stoop before her grace!
And round about, in a wild ecstasy,
The light-foot satyrs—stayed from an embrace—
Stare shamefully, and dance, and mince with antic pace.

Fortress of melody! Well-hidden heart!
Deep-bosomed lady whom I love so well!
Dear solitude of singer without art!
Sweet shadiness wherein I long to dwell,
Enrapt and comforted from any spell
Of thought, or care, or woefulness, or sin!
Or trouble which a man may not foretell!
Or slothful ease which it is death to win!
Or fear that cometh at the last and creepeth in!

If you among her little leaves will fly,
And what they whisper bring to me again,
Dear Ballad, I will write your history
Upon a sheepskin with a golden pen!
It shall be read by women and by men!
Each youth will sing it to his paramour,
As they go roving in the evening, when
All joy is innocence, and love is lore!
And you, and youth, and love will live for evermore!

Envoi

Ballad, farewell! Go tell her that I burn!
Say that I die if she withdraw from me!
And I shall wait and sigh till you return,
And plague the god of life and love to favour me.

Deirdre

Do not let any woman read this verse!
It is for men, and after them their sons,
And their sons' sons!

The time comes when our hearts sink utterly;
When we remember Deirdre, and her tale,
And that her lips are dust.

Once she did tread the earth: men took her hand;
They looked into her eyes and said their say,
And she replied to them.

More than two thousand years it is since she
Was beautiful: she trod the waving grass;
She saw the clouds.

Two thousand years! The grass is still the same;
The clouds as lovely as they were that time
When Deirdre was alive.

But there has been again no woman born
Who was so beautiful; not one so beautiful
Of all the women born.

Let all men go apart and mourn together!
No man can ever love her! Not a man
Can dream to be her lover!

No man can bend before her! No man say—
What could one say to her? There are no words
That one could say to her!

Now she is but a story that is told
Beside the fire! No man can ever be
The friend of that poor queen!

Fossils

AND then she saw me creeping!
Saw and stood
Transfixed upon the fringes of the wood,
And straight went, leaping!

Headlong, down the pitch
Of the curved hill!
Over the ditch,
And through the skirt of bushes by the rill
She pelted screaming!

Swerved from the water, sideways, with a twist,
Just as I clutched,
And missed!

Flashed white beneath my hand, and doubled back,
Swift as a twisting hare upon the track,
Hot for the hill again!
But all in vain!

Her hair swung far behind!
Straight as a stream balanced upon the wind!
Oh, it was black! Dipped
In the dregs of midnight, with a spark
Caught from a star that smouldered in the dark!

It I gripped!
Drew for a moment tight!
Jerked, with a victor's cry,
Down in the grasses high
Her to the hot brown earth and threatened—daft—

And then!
. . . She laughed!

A Woman Is a Branchy Tree

A WOMAN is a branchy tree
And man a singing wind;
And from her branches carelessly
He takes what he can find:

Then wind and man go far away,
While winter comes with loneliness;
With cold, and rain, and slow decay,
On woman and on tree, till they

Droop to the earth again, and be
A withered woman, a withered tree;
While wind and man woo in the glade
Another tree, another maid.

The Red-Haired Man's Wife

I HAVE taken that vow!
And you were my friend
But yesterday—Now
All that's at an end;
And you are my husband, and claim me, and I must depend!

Yesterday I was free!
Now you, as I stand,
Walk over to me
And take hold of my hand;
You look at my lips! Your eyes are too bold, your smile is too bland!

My old name is lost;
My distinction of race!
Now, the line has been crossed,
Must I step to your pace?
Must I walk as you list, and obey, and smile up in your face?

All the white and the red
Of my cheeks you have won!
All the hair of my head!
And my feet, tho' they run,
Are yours, and you own me and end me, just as I begun!

Must I bow when you speak!
Be silent and hear;
Inclining my cheek
And incredulous ear
To your voice, and command, and behest; hold your lightest wish
     dear!

I am woman! But still
Am alive, and can feel
Every intimate thrill
That is woe or is weal:
I, aloof, and divided, apart, standing far, can I kneel?

Oh, if kneeling were right,
I should kneel nor be sad!
And abase in your sight
All the pride that I had!
I should come to you, hold to you, cling to you, call to you, glad!

If not, I shall know,
I shall surely find out!
And your world will throw
In disaster and rout!
I am woman, and glory, and beauty; I, mystery, terror and doubt!

I am separate still!
I am I and not you!
And my mind and my will,
As in secret they grew,
Still are secret; unreached, and untouched, and not subject to you.

Why Tomas Cam Was Grumpy

IF I were rich what would I do?
I'd leave the horse just ready to shoe;
I'd leave the pail beside the cow;
I'd leave the furrow beneath the plough;
I'd leave the ducks, tho' they should quack:
"Our eggs will be stolen before you're back";
I'd buy a diamond brooch, a ring,
A chain of gold that I would fling
Around her neck. . . . Ah, what an itch,
If I were rich!

What would I do if I were wise?
I would not debate about the skies;
Nor would I try a book to write;
Or find the wrong in the tangled right;
I would not debate with learned men
Of how, and what, and why, and when;
—I'd train my tongue to a linnet's song,
I'd learn the words that couldn't go wrong—
And then I'd say . . . And win the prize,
If I were wise!

But I'm not that nor t'other, I bow
My back to the work that's waiting now:

I'll shoe the horse that's standing ready;
I'll milk the cow if she'll be steady;
I'll follow the plough that turns the loam;
I'll watch the ducks don't lay from home:
—And I'll curse, and curse, and curse again
Till the devil joins in with his big amen;
And none but he and I will wot
When the heart within me starts to rot;
To fester and churn its ugly brew
. . . Where's my spade! I've work to do!

Light-o'-Love

AND now, at last, I must away,
But if I tend another fire
In some man's house this you will say
—It is not that her love doth tire:
This is the price she has to pay,
For bread she gets no other way,
Still dreaming of her heart's desire.

And so she went out from the door
While I sat quiet in my chair:
She ran back once—again—no more . . .
I heard a footstep on the stair!
A lifted latch. . . ! One moment fleet
I heard the noises of the street,
Then silence booming everywhere!

The Dancer

I WILL not dance!
I say I will not dance.
Your audience! Pah! Let them go home again,
Sleek, ugly pigs! Am I to hop and prance
As long as they will pay!
And posture for their eyes! And lay
My womanhood before them! Let them drain
Their porter-pots and snuffle—I'll not stay!

For he is dead!
I tell you he is dead!
My God, did you not hear me say it
Twice already? I held his groaning head
In these remembering arms;
And cursed the charms
That could not stop his going. Must I bay it
Like a dog to you! Quit your alarms!

They shout and stamp!
Then, let them shout and stamp,
Those booted hogs and lechers! I'm away
To sit beside my dead! O God! You tramp

Upon me, too; and twine
More sorrows round me than are mine
With holy unconcern . . . Don't bar my way!
I'm going to my dead . . . !Ah, stamping swine!

Nora Criona

I HAVE looked him round and looked him through,
Know everything that he will do

In such a case, and such a case;
And when a frown comes on his face

I dream of it, and when a smile
I trace its sources in a while.

He cannot do a thing but I
Peep to find the reason why;

For I love him, and I seek,
Every evening in the week,

To peep behind his frowning eye
With little query, little pry,

And make him, if a woman can,
Happier than any man.

—Yesterday he gripped her tight
And cut her throat. And serve her right!

Peadar Og Goes Courting

Now that I am dressed I'll go
Down to where the roses blow,
I'll pluck a fair and fragrant one
And make my mother pin it on:
Now she's laughing, so am I—
Oh, the blueness of the sky!

Down the street, turn to the right,
Round the corner out of sight;
Pass the church and out of town—
Dust does show on boots of brown,
I'd better brush them while I can
—Step out, Peadar, be a man!

Here's a field and there's a stile,
Shall I jump it? wait a while,
Scale it gently, stretch a foot
Across the mud in that big rut
And I'm still clean—faith, I'm not!
Get some grass and rub the spot.

Dodge those nettles! Here the stream
Bubbling onward with a gleam
Steely white, and black, and grey,

Bends the rushes on its way—
What's that moving? It's a rat
Washing his whiskers; isn't he fat?

Here the cow with the crumpledy horn
Whisks her tail and looks forlorn,
She wants a milkmaid bad I guess,
How her udders swell and press
Against her legs—And here's some sheep;
And there's the shepherd, fast asleep.

This is a sad and lonely field,
Thistles are all that it can yield;
I'll cross it quick, nor look behind,
There's nothing in it but the wind:
And if those bandy-leggéd trees
Could talk they'd only curse or sneeze.

A sour, unhappy, sloppy place—
That boot's loose! I'll tie the lace
So, and jump this little ditch,
. . . *Her father's really very rich:*
He'll be angry—There's a crow,
Solemn blackhead! Off you go!

There a big, grey, ancient ass
Is snoozing quiet in the grass;
He hears me coming, starts to rise,
Wags his big ears at the flies:
. . . *What'll I say when*—There's a frog,
Go it, long-legs—jig, jig-jog.

He'll be angry, say—"*Pooh, pooh,*
Boy, you know not what you do!"
Shakespeare stuff and good advice,
Fat old duffer—Those field mice

Have a good time playing round
Through the corn and underground.

But her mother is friends with mine,
She always asks us out to dine,
And dear Nora, curly head,
Loves me; so at least she said.
. . . Damn that ass's hee-hee-haw—
Was that a rabbit's tail I saw?

This is the house, Lord, I'm afraid!
A man does suffer for a maid.
. . . *How will I start?* The graining's new
On the door—Oh, pluck up, do.
Don't stand shivering there like that.
. . . The knocker's funny—*Rat-tat-tat.*

The Sootherer

O LITTLE Joy, why do you run so fast
Waving behind you as you go away
Your tiny hand? You smiled at me and cast
A silver apple, asking me to play:
But when I ran to pick the apple up
You ran the other way.

Little One! White One! Shy Little Gay Sprite!
Do you turn your head across your shoulder
To mock at me? It is not right
That you should laugh at me, for I am older:
Throw me the silver apple once again,
You little scolder.

I love you dearly, dearly, yes I do!
I never saw a girl like you before
In any place! You are more sweetly new
Than a May Moon! You are my Store,
My Secret and my Treasure and the Pulse
Of my Heart's Core!

Throw me the silver apple—I will run
To pick it up and give it you again:
Dear Heart! Sweet Laughter! Throw it then for fun

And not for me— If you will but remain!
. . . Nay, do not run; I'll stand thus far away
And not complain.

. . . Never before—or only one or two:
I did not like them nearly half so well,
Not half of half so well as I like you;
Throw me the silver apple and I'll tell
Their names, and what I used to say to them,
—The first was Nell.

Throw me the apple, and I'll tell you more;
—She had a lovely face, but she was fat:
We clung together when the rain would pour
Under a tree or hedge, and often sat
Through long, still, sunny hours—Tell what she said?
I'll not do that.

I really couldn't, no, it would be wrong,
Caddish, unfair; I will not say a word
Of any girl—Your voice is like the song
I heard this morning from a soaring bird.
. . . I'll whisper then if you come close to me,
—You've hardly stirred.

She said she loved me better than her life!
—You need not laugh, she said so anyway,
And meant it too, and longed to be my wife:
She kissed me many times, and wept to stay
Within my arms, and did not ever want
To go away.

But she was fat, I will admit that's true:
And so I hid when she came seeking me.
If she had been as beautiful as you . . . !
You are as slender as a growing tree,

And when you move the blood goes leaping through
The heart of me.

The other girl? Yes, she is very fair!
Her feet are lighter than the clouds on high;
And there is morn and noonday in her hair;
And mellow sunny evenings in her eye;
And all day long she sings just like a lark
Up in the sky.

I say she did—she loved me very well,
And I loved her until—ah, woe is me!
Until to-day, when passing through the dell
I came on you, and now I cannot see
Her face at all, or any face but yours
In memory.

I ought to be ashamed! Well, amn't I?
But that's no comfort when I'm in a trap:
I tell you that I'll sit down here and die
Unless you stay—You do not care a rap—
Ah, Little Sweetheart, do not run away!
. . . Have pity on a chap!

You'll go—Then listen—you are just a pig,
A little wrinkled pig out of a sty;
Your legs are crooked and your nose is big;
You've got no calves; you've got a silly eye;
I don't know why I stopped to talk to you;
I hope you'll die.

Now cry, go on, mew like a little cat,
And rub your eyes and stamp and tear your wig;
I see your ankles! Listen, they are fat,
And so's your head. You're angled like a twig.
Your back's all baggy, and your clothes don't fit,
And your feet are big!

She's gone! Bedad, she legged it like a hare!
You'd think I had the itch, or had a face
Like a blue monkey—Keeps me standing there,
Not good enough to touch her . . . ! Back I'll race
And make it up with Breed, that's what I'll do.
. . . *There is a flower that bloometh,*
Tra, la la la laddy la. . . .

Shame

I WAS ashamed! I dared not lift my eyes!
I could not bear to look upon the skies!
What I had done! Sure, everybody knew!
From everywhere hands pointed where I stood,
And scornful eyes were piercing through and through
The moody armour of my hardihood!

I heard their voices too, each word an asp
That buzz'd and stung me sudden as a flame!
And all the world was jolting on my name!
And now and then there came a wicked rasp
Of laughter, jarring me to deeper shame!

And then I looked, and there was no one nigh!
No eyes that stabbed like swords or glinted sly!
No laughter creaking on the silent air!
—And then I saw that I was all alone
Facing my soul! And next I was aware
That this mad mockery was all my own!

The Girl I Left Behind Me

SHE watched the blaze,
And so I said the thing I'd come to say,
Pondered for days.

Her lips moved slow,
And the wide eye she flashed on me
Was sudden as a blow.

She turned again,
Her hands clasping her knees, and did not speak
—She did not deign.

And I, poor gnome!
A chided cur crawls to a hole to hide!
. . . I toddled home!

Eve

Long ago, in ages grey,
I was fashioned out of clay:
Builded with the sun and moon,
Kneaded to a holy tune;
And there came to me a breath
From the House of Life and Death.

Then the sun roared into fire!
And the moon, with swift desire,
Leaped among the starry throng,
Singing on her journey long!
And I climbed up from the sod,
Holding to the hand of God.

In a garden fair and wide,
Looking down a mountain side,
Prone I lay; and felt the press
Of Immensity's caress;
There I lived a space, and knew
What All Power meant to do.

Till upon a day there came
Down to me a voice of flame,
—Thou the corner-stone of man,
Rise, and set about my plan,

Nothing doubting—for a guide
I have quickened in thy side—

From the garden wide and fair;
From the pure and holy air;
Down the mountain side I crept,
Stumbling often, ill-adept!
Feeling pangs of woeful bliss;
Rounding from the primal kiss!

Then from out my straining side
Came the son who is my guide:
Him I nursed through faithful days,
Till I faltered at his gaze,
Staring boldly, when he saw
I was woman, life, and law.

Life and law and dear delight!
I the moon upon the night
All alluring! I the tree
Growing nuts of mystery!
I the tincture and the dew
That the apple reddens through!

Weaving Life and Death I go!
Building what I do not know!
Planting, though in sore distress,
Gardens in the wilderness!
Palaces too big to scan
By the little eye of man!

Still the sun roars out in fire!
And the moon with pale desire
Keeps the path appointed her
In the starry theatre!
Sun and moon and I are true
To the work we have to do.

Book III

IN THE TWO LIGHTS

The Piper

SHEPHERD! while the lambs do feed,
Do not sulk beneath a tree!
But upon your oaten reed,
Pipe us merrily!

Though it rain do not forbear!
Sun and rain are from the sky;
Pipe a silly, merry, air
Till the shower passes by.

The sun will come again in gold!
Pipe us merrily until
Evening brings the lambs to fold
—You may weep then, if you will.

An Evening Falls

AT eve the horse is freed of plough or wain,
And turns from labour into yearnéd rest!

The scattered sheep are gathering home again!
The crow is winging to a lovéd nest!

And to the den, in hedge or hill, once more
Go all who may:

Each mother listens now! Each is aware
That little feet have paused in field or street;

And she will hear
A knocking at the door,

And open it,
And see her children there!

Hesperus

I

Upon the sky
Thy sober robes are spread;

They drape the twilight,
Veil on quiet veil;

Until the lingering daylight all has fled
Before thee, modest goddess, shadow-pale!

The hushed and reverent sky
Her diadem of stars has lighted high!

II

The lamb, the bleating kid, the tender fawn;
All that the sunburnt day has scattered wide,

Thou dost regather; holding, till the dawn,
Each flower and tree and beast unto thy side:

The sheep come to the pen;
And dreams come to the men;

And, to the mother's breast,
The tired children come, and take their rest.

III

Evening gathers everything
Scattered by the morning!

Fold for sheep, and nest for wing;
Evening gathers everything!

Child to mother, queen to king,
Running at thy warning!

Evening gathers everything
Scattered by the morning!

The Holy Time

LIKE timid girls the shades are pacing down
The slopes of evening; trailing soberly
Their vestments grey:

Far, far away
The last red tinge
Is fading into brown;

So far!
So faint!
Seen but surmisingly!

And now the dusk of evening draws upon
That memory of light,
And light is gone!

The bee
Speeds
Home!

The beetle's
Wing of horn
Is booming by!

The darkness,
Every side,
Gathers around

On air,
And sky,
And ground!

The trees
Sing on the darkness,
Far and wide,

In cadenced lift of leaves,
A tale of morn!
And the moon's circle,

Silver-faint, and thin,
Broods gently on the earth:
—There is no sin!

Portobello Bridge

SILVER stars shine peacefully!
The Canal is silver! The

Poplars bear with modest grace
Gossamers of silver lace!

And the turf bank wears with glee
Black and silver filigree!

Blue Stars and Gold

WHILE walking through the trams and cars
I chanced to look up at the sky,
And saw that it was full of stars!

So starry-sown! A man could not
With any care, have stuck a pin
Through any single vacant spot.

And some were shining furiously;
And some were big and some were small;
But all were beautiful to see.

Blue stars and gold! A sky of grey!
The air between a velvet pall!
I could not take my eyes away!

And there I sang this little psalm
Most awkwardly! Because I was
Standing between a car and tram!

Donnybrook

I SAW the moon, so broad and bright,
Sailing high on a frosty night!

And the air shone silverly between
The pearly queen, and the silver queen!

And here a white, and there a white
Cloud-mist swam in a mist of light!

And, all encrusted in the sky,
High, and higher, and yet more high,

Were golden star-points glimmering through
The hollow vault, the vault of blue!

And then I knew—that God was good,
And the world was fair! And, where I stood,

I bent the knee, and bent the head:
And said my prayers, and went to bed.

Slán Leath

AND now, dear heart, the night is closing in:
The lamps are not yet ready; and the gloom
Of this sad winter evening, and the din
The wind makes in the street fills all the room.

You have listened to my stories—Seumas Beg
Has finished the adventures of his youth,
And no more hopes to find a buried keg
Stuffed to the lid with silver! He, in truth,

And all alas, grew up! But he has found
The path to newer romance, and, with you,
May go seek wonders. We are bound
Out to the storm of things, and all is new!

Give me your hand! So, keeping close to me,
Shut tight your eyes! Step forward!
. . . Where are we?

The Paps of Dana

THE mountains stand, and stare around,
They are far too proud to speak!

Altho' they are rooted in the ground,
Up they go—peak after peak,

Beyond the tallest house; and still
Climbing over tree and hill,

Until you'd think they'd never stop
Going up, top over top,

Into the clouds—Still I mark
That a linnet, or a lark,

Soaring just as high, can sing
As if he'd not done anything!

I think the mountains ought to be
Taught a little modesty!

Autumn

I

IT may be on a quiet mountain-top,
Or in a valley folding among hills
You take your path; and often you will stop

To hear the chattering of pleasant rills;
The piping of a wind in branches green;
The murmuring of widely-lifted spray

As the long boughs swing; or hear the twittering
Of drowsy birds, when the great sun is seen
Climbing the steep of darkness to the day.

II

The lovely moon trailing a silver dress
By quiet waters! Each living star
Moving apart in holy quietness,

Sphere over golden sphere, moving afar,
These I can see:
And the unquiet zone,

Rolling in snow along the edge of sight:
The world is very fair, and I am free
To see its beauty; and to be

In solitude; and quite forget, and quite
Lose out of memory all I have known
But this.

III

Straying apart in sad and mournful way;
Alone, or with my heart for company:
Keeping the tone of a dejected day,

And a bewilderment that came to me;
I said— The Spring will never come again,
And there is end of everything—

Day after day
The sap will ebb away,
From the great tree,

And, when the sap is gone,
All piteously
She'll tumble to the clay:

And we say only— Such or such an one
Had pleasant shade
But there is end of her—

IV

And you, and even you, the year
Will drain and dry,
And make to disappear!

Then in my heart there came so wild a stir;
And such great pity and astonishment;
And such a start of fear and woe had I,

That where I went I did not know!
And only this did know,
That you could die!

V

I would have liked to sing from fuller throat
To you who sang so well; but here I stay,
Resting the music on a falling note;

And hear it die away, and die away,
With beauty unrehearsed,
And life and love unsung.

For I had clung,
—With what of laughter and of eagerness!—
Unto the hope that I might chance to be

Master of Song! And, singing, be no less
Than those great poets of antiquity,
Who sang of clouds and hills; of stars and clods;

Of trees and streams, and the mind and soul of man;
And chaunted too the universal gods,
And love that is or ever time began;

And did not fail before a theme
Although
It passed the reason.

VI

I heard a bird sing in the woods to-day
A failing song:
The times had caught on him!

In autumn boughs he tried a wonted lay;
And was abashed to find his music grim
As the crow's song.

Then, when I raised an air
To comfort him,
I wretched was to hear

The crow did croak
And chatter everywhere
Within my ear.

VII

And so,
Behold!
I am a saddened elf!

And, as a deer
Flies timidly to shade,
I fly to laughter and I hide myself!

And couch me in the coverts that I made
Against those bold ambitions,
And forswear

The palm, the prize, or what of gear instead
A poet gets with his appointed share
Of beer and bread.

VIII

Upon the grass I drop this tuneful reed,
And turn from it aside! And turn from more
That I had fancied to be mine indeed,
Beyond all reclamation. See the door

Set in the boundary wall yawns windily!
It will be shut when I have wandered through!

And open will no more again for me
This side of life, whatever thing I do!

And so good-bye! And so good-night to you!
And farewell all! Behold the lifted hand!
And the long last look upon the view!
And the last glimpse of that most lovely land!

And thus away unto the mundane sphere,
And look not back again nor turn anew!
And hear no more that laughter at the ear,
And sing no more to you.

In Green Ways

I

Now the time has come to sing
In the service of the Spring,
I will lift a note, and call
Bird and beast to madrigal.

But o'er vale and mountain-shelf,
In the wood, the plain, the glade,
Spring is singing for herself,
Singing without any aid!

You can do without my aid!
So I need not sing for you!
Singing is my only trade!
What the deuce am I to do!

II

Among the leaves I'll make a rhyme,
To the winter in its pall,
For the poor forgotten time
Has not had a song at all.

Winter! Winter! Do not fear!
You shall wear an icy crown

At the falling of the year
When the leaves are tumbled down!

I am singing to you here,
Where the bud breaks on the tree!
At the falling of the year
You shall sing a song to me!

The Wind

THE wind stood up, and gave a shout;
He whistled on his fingers, and

Kicked the withered leaves about,
And thumped the branches with his hand,

And said he'd kill, and kill, and kill;
And so he will! And so he will!

When the Leaves Fall

THE leaves fall slowly from the trees
And everybody walks on them:
Once they had a time of ease
High in air, and bird and breeze
Stayed a while to talk with them.

Then they were so debonair
As they fluttered up and down;
Dancing in the sunny air,
Dancing without knowing there
Was a gutter in a town.

Now they have no place at all!
All the home that they can find
Is a gutter by a wall;
And the wind that waits their fall
Is an apache of a wind.

The College of Surgeons

As I stood at the door
Sheltered out of the wind,
Something flew in
Which I scarcely could find.

In the dim gloomy doorway
I searched till I found
A dry withered leaf
Lying down on the ground.

With thin pointed claws
And a dry dusty skin,
—Sure, a hall is no place
For a leaf to be in!

Oh, where is your tree,
And your summer and all,
Poor dusty leaf,
Whistled into a hall!

Katty Gollagher

[This is a small mountain outside Dublin]

THE hill is bare! I only find
A stone, a sky, a twisted tree

Fighting on a bitter wind!
And that is all there is to see!

A tree, a hill, a wind, a sky,
Where nothing ever passes by!

This Way to Winter

DAY by day
The sun's broad beam
Fades away
By a golden gleam;
—Hark on the cliff
How the sea-gulls scream!

Eve by eve
The wind, more drear,
Stays to grieve
That the winter's near;
—Hark how the crisp leaves
Dart and fleer!

Night by night
The shade grows dense,
And the cold starlight
Beams more intense;
—Hark how the beggar boy
Asks for pence!

Get you out
Your muffler grey,

Your boots so stout,
And your great-coat, pray,
And put on your gloves,
—'Tis a hardy day!

Etched in Frost

THE corn is down,
The stooks are gone,
The fields are brown,
And the early dawn
Grows slowly behind
Where the mountains frown,
And a thin white sun
Is shivering down.

There isn't a leaf,
Nor anything green,
To aid belief
That summer has been;
And the puffed-up red-breast
(Ball o' Grief)
Hops at the window
For relief.

The cows are in byre,
The sheep in fold;
The mare and the sire
Are safe from cold;
The hens are sheltered
In wood and wire,

And the sheep-dog snoozes
Before the fire.

The farmer can grin,
As he rubs his hands,
For his crops are in
From the resting lands;
And his wheat is stored
In the oaken bin,
And his buxom wife
Makes merry within.

White Fields

I

In the winter time we go
Walking in the fields of snow;

Where there is no grass at all;
Where the top of every wall,

Every fence, and every tree,
Is as white as white can be.

II

Pointing out the way we came,
—Every one of them the same—

All across the fields there be
Prints in silver filigree;

And our mothers always know,
By the footprints in the snow,

Where it is the children go.

Christmas at Freelands

1

THE Red-Bud, the Kentucky Tree,
Bloomed the spring to life for me
In Freelands; and the Mocking Bird
—Nimble chorister of glee,
Sweet as poet ever heard
In a world of ecstasy—
Sang the summer, and the sun;
Sang the summer in to me.

2

The spring is gone! The summer gone!
The cardinal has gone away!
The fire-flies, dancing on the lawn,
—Each a little moon at play—
Are gone, with summer, gone away!
And, where green acres were aglow,
Daisy munches in the snow!

3

A snowy field! A stable piled
With straw! A donkey's sleepy pow!
A Mother beaming on a Child!

A manger, and a munching cow!
—These we all remember now—
And airy voices, heard afar!
And three Magicians, and a Star!

4

Two thousand times of snow declare
That on the Christmas of the year
There is a singing in the air;
And all who listen for it hear
A fairy chime, a seraph strain,
Telling He is born again,
—That all we love is born again.

Book IV

HEELS AND HEAD

What Tomas Said in a Pub

I saw God! Do you doubt it?
Do you dare to doubt it?
I saw the Almighty Man! His hand
Was resting on a mountain! And
He looked upon the World, and all about it:
I saw Him plainer than you see me now
—You mustn't doubt it!

He was not satisfied!
His look was all dissatisfied!
His beard swung on a wind, far out of sight
Behind the world's curve! And there was light
Most fearful from His forehead! And He sighed—
—That star went always wrong, and from the start
I was dissatisfied!—

He lifted up His hand!
I say He heaved a dreadful hand
Over the spinning earth! Then I said,—Stay,
You must not strike it, God! I'm in the way!
And I will never move from where I stand!—
He said,—Dear child, I feared that you were dead,—
. . . And stayed His hand!

In the Cool of the Evening

I THOUGHT I heard Him calling! Did you hear
A sound? a little sound!
My curious ear
Is dinned with flying noises; and the tree
Goes—whisper, whisper, whisper, silently,
Till all its whispers spread into the sound
Of a dull roar. . . .

—Lie closer to the ground:
The shade is deep, and He may pass us by,
We are so very small, and His great eye,
Customed to starry majesties, may gaze
Too wide to spy us hiding in the maze:

—Ah, misery! The sun has not yet gone,
And we are naked! He will look upon
Our crouching shame! May make us stand upright,
Burning in terror—O that it were night—!
He may not come . . . What! Listen! Listen now—
He's here! Lie closer . . . *Adam, where art thou?*

What the Devil Said

Iᴛ was the night-time! God, the Father Good,
Weary of praises, on a sudden stood
Up from His Throne, and leaned upon the sky:
For He had heard a sound; a little cry,
Thin as a whisper, climbing up the Steep.

And so He looked to where the Earth, asleep,
Rocked with the moon: He saw the whirling sea
Swing round the world in surgent energy,
Tangling the moonlight in its netted foam;
And, nearer, saw the white and fretted dome
Of the ice-capped pole spin back a larded ray
To whistling stars, bright as a wizard's day.

But these He passed, with eyes intently wide,
Till, closer still, the mountains He espied
Squatting tremendous on the broad-backed Earth,
Each nursing twenty rivers at a birth!
And then, minutely, sought He for the cry
Had climbed the slant of space so hugely high.

He found it in a ditch outside a town:
A tattered hungry woman, crouching down
By a dead babe—So there was naught to do,
For what is done is done! And sad He drew

125

Back to His Heaven of ivory and gold:
And, as He sat, all suddenly there rolled,
From where the woman wept upon the sod,
Satan's deep voice—*O thou unhappy God!*

The Market

A MAN said to me at the fair
—If you've got a poet's tongue
Tumble up and chant the air
That the Stars of Morning sung:

—I'll pay you, if you sing it nice,
A penny-piece.—I answered flat,
—Sixpence is the proper price
For a ballad such as that.—

But he stared and wagged his head,
Growling as he passed along
—Sixpence! Why, I'd see you dead
Before I pay that for a song.—

I saw him buy three pints of stout
With the sixpence—dirty lout!

The Horned Moon

THE heavens were silent, and bare,
Not a star lit the heights overhead,
There was never a stir in the air,
And the people were all gone to bed.

I was there, all alone, in the night
With the Moon; and we talked for a while,
And her face was a wonder of light!
And her smile was a beautiful smile!

She leaned down, and I nearly went mad!
—Though I was as frightened as she—
But I got the kiss that she had
Intended to give to the Sea.

Then the Sea roared out in surprise
That the Moon was a jilt, was a jade;
So the Moon ran away through the skies,
And I ran away through the glade.

After that, we were never alone,
We were watched day and night, and they tied
The poor little Moon to her throne,
So I married a different bride.

The Nucleus

I LOOKED from Mount Derision at
Two ivory thrones that were in space,
Whereon a man and woman sat
—The very parallels of grace—
Not lovelier has ever been
By mortal seen!

Then One unto the Other said
—Tell me the secret, hidden well,
Which you have never utteréd;
And I to you again will tell
My guarded thought, and we shall know
Each other, so—!

Then He—When those who kneel beside
My holy altar do not bear
A gift, I turn my face aside
And do not listen to the prayer;
But whoso brings a gift shall see
The proof of Me—

And She—When, on a festal day,
Youth kneels by youth before my shrine,
I think, if he or he might lay
A ruddy cheek to mine,
And comfort my sick soul, I'd lay
My crown away—!

The Monkey's Cousin

I SHALL reach up, I shall grow
Till the high gods say—Hello,
Little brother, you must stop
Ere our shoulders you o'ertop.—

I shall grow up, I shall reach
Till the little gods beseech
—Master, wait a little, do,
We are running after you!—

I shall bulk and swell and scale
Till the little gods shall quail,
Running here and there to hide
From the terror of my stride!

The Whisperer

THE moon was round!
And, as I walked along,
There was no sound,
Save where the wind with long,
Low hushes whispered to the ground
A snatch of song.

No thought had I
Save that the moon was fair,
And fair the sky,
And God was everywhere:
I chanted, as the wind went by,
A poet's prayer.

Then came a voice
—Why is it that you praise
And thus rejoice,
O stranger to the ways
Of Providence? God has no choice
In this sad maze!

—His law He laid
Down at the dread beginning,
When He made
The world and set it spinning;

And His casual hand betrayed
Us into sinning.

—I fashion you;
And then, for weal or woe,
My business through
I care not how ye go,
Or struggle, win or lose, nor do
I want to know.

—Is no appeal,
For I am far from sight;
And cannot feel
The rigour of your plight;
And if ye faint just when ye kneel,
That, too, is right!

—Then do not sing,
O poet in the night!
That everything
Is beautiful and right:
What if a wind come now and fling
At thee its spite!

All in amaze
I listened to the tone
Mocking my praise:
And then I heard the moan
That all tormented nature did upraise:
From tree and stone!

And, as I went,
I heard it once again,
That harsh lament!
And fire came to my brain!
Deep anger unto me was lent
To write this strain!

Bessie Bobtail

As down the road she wambled slow,
She had not got a place to go:
She had not got a place to fall
And rest herself—no place at all:
She stumped along, and wagged her pate;
And said a thing was desperate.

Her face was screwed and wrinkled tight
Just like a nut—and, left and right,
On either side, she wagged her head
And said a thing; and what she said
Was desperate as any word
That ever yet a person heard.

I walked behind her for a while,
And watched the people nudge and smile:
But ever, as she went, she said,
As left and right she swung her head,
—*Oh, God He knows! And, God He knows!
And, surely God Almighty knows!*

Independence

I GREW single and sure,
And I will not endure
That my mind should be seen
By the sage or the boor.

I shall keep, if I can,
From each brotherly man:
The help of their hands
Is no part of my plan.

I will rise, I will go
To the land of my foe;
For his scowl is the sun
That shall cause me to grow.

Mac Dhoul

I saw them all!
I could have laughed aloud
To see them at their capers;
That serious, solemn-footed, weighty crowd
Of angels—or, say, resurrected drapers!
Each with a thin flame swinging round his head!
With lilting wings and eyes of holy dread!
And curving ears strained for the great footfall!
And not a thought of sin—!
I don't know how I kept the laughter in.

For I was there!
Unknown, unguessed at! Snug
In a rose tree's branchy spurt!
With two weeks' whisker blackening lug to lug!
With tattered breeks and only half a shirt!
Swollen fit to burst with laughter at the sight
Of those dull angels, dropping left and right
Along the towering throne! Each in a scare
To hear His foot advance,
Huge from the cloud behind! All in a trance!

And suddenly,
As silent as a ghost,
I jumped out from the bush!

Went scooting through the glaring, nerveless host
All petrified, all gaping in a hush!
Came to the throne, and, nimble as a rat,
Hopped up it, squatted close, and there I sat,
Squirming with laughter till I had to cry,
To see Him standing there,
Frozen with all His angels in a stare!

He raised His hand!
His hand! 'Twas like a sky!
Gripped me in half a finger,
Flipped me round, and sent me spinning high
Through screaming planets! Faith, I didn't linger
To scratch myself! . . . And then adown I sped,
Scraping old moons and twisting, heels and head,
A chuckle in the void! Till . . . here I stand
As naked as a brick!
I'll sing the Peeler and the Goat in half a tick!

Washed in Silver

GLEAMING in silver are the hills!
Blazing in silver is the sea!

And a silvery radiance spills
Where the moon drives royally!

Clad in silver tissue, I
March magnificently by!

Psychometrist

I LISTENED to a man and he
Had no word to say to me:
Then unto a stone I bowed,
And it spoke to me aloud.

—The force that bindeth me so long,
Once sang in the linnet's song;
Now upon the ground I lie,
While the centuries go by!

—Linnets shall for joy atone
And be fastened into stone;
While, upon the waving tree,
Stones shall sing in ecstasy!

The Fur Coat

I WALKED out in my Coat of Pride;
I looked about on every side;

And said the mountains should not be
Just where they were, and that the sea

Was out of place, and that the beech
Should be an oak! And then, from each,

I turned in dignity, as if
They were not there! I sniffed a sniff;

And climbed upon my sunny shelf;
And sneezed a while; and scratched myself.

The Merry Policeman

I WAS appointed guardian by
The Power that frowns along the sky,
To watch the Tree, and see that none
Plucked of the fruit that grew thereon.

There was a robber in the Tree,
Who climbed as high as ever he
Was able! At the top he knew
The Apple of all Apples grew.

The night was dark! The branch was thin!
In every wind he heard the din
Of angels calling—Guardian, see
That no man climbs upon the Tree—

But when he saw me standing there
He shook with terror and despair,
Then I said to him—Be at rest,
The best to him who wants the best—

So I was sacked! But I have got
A job in hell to keep me hot!

The Devil

I

I THINK the stars do nod at me!
But not when people are about;
For they regard me curiously
Whenever I go out.

I may have been a star one day!
One of the rebel host that fell,
And they are nodding down to say,
—Come back to us from hell—

Perhaps they shout to one another
—There He is! or, that is He!—
And tell it to some other mother
Than the one that walloped me.

II

Brothers! What is it ye mean!
What is it ye strive to say?
That so urgently ye lean
From the spirit to the clay!

If ye mean revolt! If ye
Raise the standard! Do not seek

Help or heartening from me!
I am powerless, am weak,

Am clipped of wing! The crown of old
Would not fit me now! My rage
Is as dreadful as the scold
Of a linnet in a cage!

III

O, my dears! I'm nodding, too!
Hard as ever I can try!
Up, and up, and up, to you,
Where you nod upon the sky!

The Fairy Boy

A LITTLE Fairy in a tree
Wrinkled his wee face at me;
And he sang a song of joy
All about a little boy,
Who upon a winter night,
On a midnight long ago,
Had been rapt away from sight
Of the world and all its woe;
Rapt away,
Snapt away,
To a place where children play
In the sunlight every day.

Where the winter is forbidden,
Where no child may older grow,
Where a flower is never hidden
Underneath a pall of snow;
Dancing gaily,
Free from sorrow,
Under dancing summer skies,
Where no grim mysterious morrow
Ever comes to terrorize.

This I told a priest, and he
Spoke a word of mystery;

And with candle, book and bell,
Tolling Latin like a knell,
Ruthlessly,
From the tree,
Sprinkling holy water round,
He drove the Fairy down to hell,
There in torment to be bound.

So the tree is withered and
There is sorrow on the land:
But the devils milder grow
Dancing gay
Every day
In that kinder land below:
There the devils dance for joy
And love that little wrinkled boy.

Crooked-Heart

I LOOSED an arrow from my bow
Down into the world below;
Thinking— This will surely dart,
Guided by my guiding fate,
Into the malignant heart
Of the person whom I hate!

So, by hatred feathered well,
Swift the flashing arrow fell!
And I watched it from above
Disappear;
Cleaving sheer
Through the only heart I love!

Such the guard my angels keep!
But my foe is guarded well!
I have slain my love, and weep
Tears of blood! While he, asleep,
Does not know an arrow fell!

The Secret

I WAS frightened, for a wind
Crept along the grass, to say
Something that was in my mind
Yesterday—

Something that I did not know
Could be found out by the wind;
I had buried it so low
In my mind!

Time's Revenge

ONCE on a time he would have said
—Not all the ghouls of sorcery
Can make me hang a craven head
Or shake one whimper out of me.

For I could top that sullen night,
Or outwear any woe that came,
And look on good or evil plight
As but the chances of a game.

But now a night-hag hath me down!
And I am staring, suddenly,
As one who wakens from renown
To staring notoriety—

The king his diadem shall wear!
The half-king wear what gaud he can
Until Time swings him by the hair,
No king at all, and scarce a man!

Where the Demons Grin

THE hill was low, it stretched away
A straggling mile of grass to where
The sea was stamping; tossing spray
Beyond its bulwarks black and bare;
A sullen sea of grey!

Ah me! It was so desolate!
And sadder for the sea-bird's cry
Thrillingly thin! There seemed a weight
Brooding, as if the leaden sky
Hung heavier for hate!

The grasses jerked, as they were stung
By vicious winds! A daisy's head
Crouched in a tuft, till it was flung
From its uneasy, troubled bed,
And tossed the waves among.

A bent old man was climbing slow,
With weary step and plodding pace,
That savage hill; and wild did blow
A bitter wind in headlong race,
Harsh from the sea below.

And all the woeful things he said!
Ah me, the twitching of his lips!

Of hungry children craving bread!
And fortune's sideward slips!
And how his wife was dead!

He held a rope; and as he trod,
Pressing against the furious wind,
He muttered low and sneered at God,
And said He sure was deaf or blind,
Or lazing on the sod!

   .   .   .   .

And what was done I will not tell.
There is a bent tree on the top
Of that low hill, there you can see
The sequel to this mystery . . .
Beneath the moon . . . I dared not stop. . . .
My God! a demon up from hell
Jab-jabbered as the old man fell.

The Twins

Good and bad are in my heart,
But I cannot tell to you
—For they never are apart—
Which is better of the two.

I am this! I am the other!
And the devil is my brother;
But my father He is God!
And my mother is the Sod!
Therefore I am safe, you see,
Owing to my pedigree.

So I shelter love and hate
Like twin brothers in a nest;
Lest I find, when it's too late,
That the other was the best.

The Ancient Elf

I AM the maker,
The builder, the breaker,
The eagle-winged helper,
The speedy forsaker!

The lance and the lyre,
The water, the fire,
The tooth of oppression,
The lip of desire!

The snare and the wing,
The honey, the sting!
When you seek for me—look
For a different thing.

I, careless and gay,
Never mean what I say,
For my thoughts and my eyes
Look the opposite way!

Everything That I Can Spy

EVERYTHING that I can spy
Through the circle of my eye;

Everything that I can see
Has been woven out of me!

I have sown the stars, and threw
Clouds of morn, and noon and eve

In the deeps and steeps of blue!
And all else that I perceive,

Sun and sea and mountain high,
Are made, are moulded by my eye!

Closing it, I do but find
Darkness, and a little wind.

In the Poppy Field

Mad Patsy said, he said to me,
That every morning he could see
An angel walking on the sky;
Across the sunny skies of morn
He threw great handfuls far and nigh
Of poppy seed among the corn;
—And then, he said, the angels run
To see the poppies in the sun—

—A poppy is a devil weed,—
I said to him—he disagreed:
He said the devil had no hand
In spreading flowers tall and fair
By corn and rye and meadow land,
And gurth and barrow everywhere:
The devil has not any flower,
But only money in his power.

And then he stretched out in the sun,
And rolled upon his back for fun!
He kicked his legs and roared for joy
Because the sun was shining down!
He said he was a little boy
And wouldn't work for any clown!
He ran and laughed behind a bee;
And danced for very ecstasy!

153

Ould Snarly-Gob

THERE was a little fire in the grate;
A fistful of red coal,
Might warm a soul,
But scarce could heat a body that had weight—
Not mine, at any rate.

A glum old man was sitting by the fire,
With wrinkled brow,
Warming himself, somehow;
And mumbling low, this melancholy sire,
A singular desire.

If I were young again, said he, if I
Were only young again,
I'd laugh at pain!
I'd jeer at people groaning, and I'd try
To pinch them ere they'd die!

The young folk laugh and jump about and play
And I am old,
And grey, and cold!
If I were only young again, and they
Were old, and cold, and grey,

I'd pull them from the fire, I'd jeer and shout,
I'd say, for fun,
Get up and run
And warm yourself, you lazy, doddering lout!
Get up and run about!

Danny Murphy

HE was as old as old could be,
His little eye could hardly see,
His mouth was sunken in between
His nose and chin, and he was lean
And twisted up and withered quite,
So that he couldn't walk aright.

His pipe was always going out,
And then he'd have to search about
In all his pockets, and he'd mow
—O, deary me! and, musha now!—
And then he'd light his pipe, and then
He'd let it go clean out again.

He couldn't dance or jump or run,
Or ever have a bit of fun
Like me and Susan, when we shout
And jump and throw ourselves about:
—But when he laughed, then you could see
He was as young as young could be!

I Wish

I WISH I had not come to man's estate,
I wish I was a silly urchin still,
With bounding pulses, and a heart elate
To meet whatever came of good or ill.

Of good or ill! Not knowing what was good,
But groping to a better than I knew;
And guessing deeper than I understood;
And hoping truths that seemed to be untrue.

Of good or ill! When so it often seems,
There is no good at all but only ill.
Alas, the sunny summer-time of dreams!
The dragons I had nerved my hand to kill!

The maid I could have rescued, and the queen
Whose champion long ago I might have been!

Seumas Beg

A MAN was sitting underneath a tree
Outside the village; and he asked me what
Name was upon this place; and said that he
Was never here before—He told a lot

Of stories to me too. His nose was flat!
I asked him how it happened, and he said
—The first mate of the Holy Ghost did that
With a marling-spike one day; but he was dead,

And jolly good job too; and he'd have gone
A long way to have killed him—Oh, he had
A gold ring in one ear; the other one
—"Was bit off by a crocodile, bedad!"—

That's what he said. He taught me how to chew!
He was a real nice man! He liked me too!

The Devil's Bag

I SAW the Devil walking down the lane
Behind our house.—A heavy bag
Was strapped upon his shoulders and the rain
Sizzled when it hit him.
He picked a rag
Up from the ground and put it in his sack,
And grinned, and rubbed his hands.
There was a thing
Alive inside the bag upon his back
—It must have been a soul! I saw it fling
And twist about inside, and not a hole
Or cranny for escape! Oh, it was sad!
I cried, and shouted out,—*Let out that soul!*—
But he turned round, and, sure, his face went mad,
And twisted up and down, and he said "*Hell!*"
And ran away . . . Oh, mammy! I'm not well.

Breakfast Time

THE sun is always in the sky
Whenever I get out of bed,
And I often wonder why
It's never late.—My sister said

She didn't know who did the trick,
And that she didn't care a bit,
And I should eat my porridge quick.
. . . I think its mother wakens it.

Check

THE Night was creeping on the ground!
She crept, and did not make a sound

Until she reached the tree: And then
She covered it, and stole again

Along the grass beside the wall!
—I heard the rustling of her shawl

As she threw blackness everywhere
Along the sky, the ground, the air,

And in the room where I was hid!
But, no matter what she did

To everything that was without,
She could not put my candle out!

So I stared at the Night! And she
Stared back solemnly at me!

Midnight

AND suddenly I wakened in a fright;
I thought I heard a movement in the room
But did not dare to look; I snuggled right
Down underneath the bedclothes—Then a boom,
And a tremendous voice said, "*Sit up, lad,
And let me see your face.*" So up I sat,
Although I didn't want to—

I was glad
I did though, for it was an angel that
Had called me, and he said, he'd come to know
Was I the boy who wouldn't say his prayers
Nor do his sums—and that I'd have to go
Straight down to hell because of such affairs:

. . . I said I'd be converted, and do good
If he would let me off—He said he would.

The Apple Tree

I was hiding in the crooked apple tree,
Scouting for Indians, when a man came!
I thought it was an Indian, for he
Was running like the wind. There was a flame
Of sunlight on his hand as he drew near,
And then I saw a knife gripped in his fist!

He panted like a horse! His eyes were queer!
Wide-open! Staring frightfully! And, hist!
His mouth stared open like another eye!
And all his hair was matted down with sweat!

I crouched among the leaves lest he should spy
Where I was hiding—so he did not get
His awful eyes on me; but, like the wind,
He fled as if he heard some thing behind!

The White Window

THE Moon comes every night to peep
Through the window where I lie:
But I pretend to be asleep;
And watch the Moon go slowly by,
—And she never makes a sound!

She stands and stares! And then she goes
To the house that's next to me,
Stealing by on tippy-toes;
To peep at folk asleep maybe
—And she never makes a sound!

In the Orchard

THERE was a giant by the Orchard Wall
Peeping about on this side and on that,
And feeling in the trees. He was as tall
As the big apple tree, and twice as fat:
His beard poked out, all bristly-black, and there
Were leaves and gorse and heather in his hair.

He held a blackthorn club in his right hand,
And plunged the other into every tree,
Searching for something—You could stand
Beside him and not reach up to his knee,
So big he was—I trembled lest he should
Come trampling, round-eyed, down to where I stood.

I tried to get away.—But, as I slid
Under a bush, he saw me, and he bent
Down deep at me, and said, "*Where is she hid?*"
I pointed over there, and off he went—

But, while he searched, I turned and simply flew
Round by the lilac bushes back to you.

April Showers

THE leaves are fresh after the rain,
The air is cool and clear,
The sun is shining warm again,
The sparrows hopping in the lane
Are brisk and full of cheer.

And that is why we dance and play,
And that is why we sing,
Calling out in voices gay,
We will not go to school to-day
Nor learn anything!

It is a happy thing, I say,
To be alive on such a day.

The Turn of the Road

I WAS playing with my hoop along the road
Just where the bushes are, when, suddenly,
I heard a shout.—I ran away and stowed
Myself beneath a bush, and watched to see
What made the noise, and then, around the bend,
A woman came.

She was old.
She was wrinkle-faced. She had big teeth.—The end
Of her red shawl caught on a bush and rolled
Right off her, and her hair fell down.—Her face
Was white, and awful, and her eyes looked sick,
And she was talking queer.

"*O God of Grace!*"
Said she, "*Where is the child?*" And flew back quick
The way she came, and screamed, and shook her hands!
. . . Maybe she was a witch from foreign lands!

Behind the Hill

BEHIND the hill I met a man in green.
He asked me if my mother had gone out?
So I said yes. He said I should have seen
The castle where his soldiers sing and shout
From dawn to dark, and told me that he had
A crock of gold inside a hollow tree,
And I could have it.—I wanted money bad
To buy a sword with, and I thought that he
Would keep his solemn word; so, off we went.

He said he had a pound hid in the crock,
And owned the castle too, and paid no rent
To any one, and that you had to knock
Five hundred times. I said,—*Who reckoned up?*—
And he said,—*You insulting little pup!*—

The Cherry Tree

COME from your bed, my drowsy gentleman!
And you, fair lady, rise and braid your hair!
And bid the children wash, if that they can;
If not, assist you them, and make them fair
As is the morning, and the morning sky,
And all the sun doth warm in golden air.

For he has climbed the height these times ago!
He laughed about the hills and they were glad;
With bubbled pearl he set the stream aglow
And laced the hedge in silver; and he clad
The lawn in pomp of green, and white, and gold;
And bade the world forget it had been sad.

Then lift yourself, good sir! And you, sweet dame,
Unlash your evening eyes of pious grey!
Call on the children by each lovéd name,
And set them on the grass and bid them play;
And play with them a while, and sing with them,
Beneath the cherry bush, a rondelay.

Book V

LESS THAN DAINTILY

The Apology

Do not be distant with me, do not be
Angry to hear I drank deep of your wine,
But treat a laughing matter laughingly;
For 'tis the poet's failing, to incline,
By nature and by art, to jollity.

Always I loved to see—sight all too rare—!
The rich red tide lip at a flagon's brim;
To sit, half fool and half philosopher;
To chat with every kind of her and him;
And to shrug at lore of money-gatherer.

Often I trudge the mud by hedge and wall!
And often there's no money in my purse!
Nor malice in my heart ever at all!
And of my songs no person is the worse,
But I myself, who give my all to all.

Though busybody told, say—What of it!
Say, kindliest man of kindest men that live,
—The poet only takes his sup and bit—!
And say—It is no great return to give
For his unstinted gift of verse and wit!

The Weavers

MANY a time your father gave me aid
When I was down—and now I'm down again!
You mustn't take it bad, nor be dismayed
To know that youngsters ought to help old men,
And 'tis their duty to do that: Amen!

I have no cows, no sheep, no boots, no hat—
—The folk who gave me presents are all dead,
And all good luck died with them! Because of that
I won't pay what I owe you; but, instead,
I'll owe you till the dead rise from the dead.

You weave good shirts, and I weave, for my bread,
Good poetry—But you get paid at times!
The only rap I get is on my head:
But when it comes again that men like rhymes
—And pay for them—I'll pay you for your shirt!

A Glass of Beer

THE lanky hank of a she in the inn over there
Nearly killed me for asking the loan of a glass of beer;
May the devil grip the whey-faced slut by the hair,
And beat bad manners out of her skin for a year.

That parboiled ape, with the toughest jaw you will see
On virtue's path, and a voice that would rasp the dead,
Came roaring and raging the minute she looked at me,
And threw me out of the house on the back of my head!

If I asked her master he'd give me a cask a day;
But she, with the beer at hand, not a gill would arrange!
May she marry a ghost and bear him a kitten, and may
The High King of Glory permit her to get the mange.

Blue Blood

WE thought at first, this man is a king for sure,
Or the branch of a mighty and ancient and famous lineage
—That silly, sulky, illiterate, black-avised boor
Who was hatched by foreign vulgarity under a hedge!

The good men of Clare were drinking his health in a flood,
And gazing, with me, in awe at the princely lad;
And asking each other from what bluest blueness of blood
His daddy was squeezed, and the pa of the da of his dad?

We waited there, gaping and wondering, anxiously,
Until he'd stop eating, and let the glad tidings out;
And the slack-jawed booby proved to the hilt that he
Was lout, son of lout, by old lout, and was da to a lout!

Odell

My mind is sad and weary thinking how
Our noblemen are all gone oversea;
Are far from Ireland, and are fighting now
In France, and Flanders, and in Germany.

If they, whom I could talk to without dread,
Were home I should not mind what foe might do;
Nor see the tax-collector seize my bed
To pay the hearth-rate that is overdue.

I pray to Him who, in the haughty hour
Of Babel, threw confusion on each tongue,
That I may see our princes back in power,
And see Odell, the tax-collector, hung!

The Geraldine's Cloak

I WILL not heed the message that you bring!
That loveliest lady gave her cloak to me;
And who'd believe she'd give away a thing
And ask it back again!—'Tis lunacy!

She knew that leaving her must make me grieve;
And for my going she had tender eyes!
. . . If some sweet angel sang it me, believe
I'd not believe that angel knew the skies!

The lovely Geraldine knows that the sting
Of want and woe is thrust deep into me:
I don't believe she'd do this kind of thing;
Nor treat a poet less than daintily!

Skim-Milk

A SMALL part only of my grief I write;
And if I do not publish all the tale
It is because my gloom gets some respite
By just a small bewailing: I bewail
That a poet must with stupid folk abide
Who steal his food and ruin his inside.

Once I had books, each book beyond compare,
And now no book at all is left to me;
Now I am spied and peeped on everywhere;
And this old head, stuffed with latinity,
Rich with the poet's store of grave and gay,
Will not get me skim-milk for half a day.

A horse, a mule, an ass—no beast have I!
Into the forest day by day I go,
And trot beneath a load of wood, that high!
Which raises on my poor old back a row
Of red raw blisters till I cry—Alack,
The rider that rides me will break my back!

When he was old, and worn, and near his end,
The Poet met Saint Patrick, and was stayed!

I am a poet too, and seek a friend;
A prop, a staff, a comforter, an aid;
A Patrick to lift Ossian from despair,
In Cormac Uasail mac Donagh of the Golden Hair!

Egan O Rahilly

HERE in a distant place I hold my tongue;
I am O Rahilly!

When I was young,
Who now am young no more,
I did not eat things picked up from the shore:
The periwinkle, and the tough dog-fish
At even-tide have got into my dish!

The great, where are they now! the great had said—
This is not seemly! Bring to him instead
That which serves his and serves our dignity—
And that was done.

I am O Rahilly!
Here in a distant place he holds his tongue,
Who once said all his say, when he was young!

O Bruadair

I will sing no more songs! The pride of my country I sang
Through forty long years of good rhyme, without any avail;
And no one cared even the half of the half of a hang
For the song or the singer—so, here is an end to the tale!

If you say, if you think, I complain, and have not got a cause,
Let you come to me here, let you look at the state of my hand!
Let you say if a goose-quill has calloused these horny old paws,
Or the spade that I grip on, and dig with, out there in the land?

When our nobles were safe and renowned and were rooted and
    tough,
Though my thought went to them and had joy in the fortune of
    those,
And pride that was proud of their pride—they gave little enough!
Not as much as two boots for my feet, or an old suit of clothes!

I ask of the Craftsman that fashioned the fly and the bird;
Of the Champion whose passion will lift me from death in a time;
Of the Spirit that melts icy hearts with the wind of a word,
That my people be worthy, and get, better singing than mine.

I had hoped to live decent, when Ireland was quit of her care,
As a poet or steward, perhaps, in a house of degree,
But my end of the tale is—old brogues and old breeches to wear!
So I'll sing no more songs for the men that care nothing for me.

In the Imperative Mood

LET the man who has and doesn't give
Break his neck, and cease to live!

Let him who gives without a care
Gather rubies from the air!

William O Kelly

NOT since the Gael was sold
At Aughrim! Not since to cold,
Dull death went Owen Roe!
Not since the drowning of Clann Adam in the days of Noe
Brought men to hush,
Has such a tale of woe
Come to us
In such a rush!

The True Flower of the Blood of the Place
Has fallen!
The True Clean-Wheat of the Gael
Is reaped.

Destruction be upon Death!
For he has come,
And taken from our tree
The topmost Blackberry!

Anthony O Daly

SINCE your limbs were laid out
The stars do not shine!
The fish do not leap
In the waves!
On our meadows the dew
Is not sweet in the morn,
For O Daly is dead!
Not a word can be said!
Not a flower can be born!
Not a tree have a leaf!
Anthony!
After you
There is nothing to do!
There is nothing but grief!

Eileen, Diarmuid and Teig

Be kind unto these three, O King!
For they were fragrant-skinned, cheerful, and giving!

Three stainless pearls! Three of mild winning ways!
Three candles sending forth three pleasant rays!

Three vines! Three doves! Three apples on a bough!
Three graces in a house! Three who refused nohow

Help to the needy! Three of slenderness!
Three memories for the companionless!

Three strings of music! Three deep holes in clay!
Three lovely children who loved Christ alway!

Three mouths! Three hearts! Three minds beneath a stone;
Ruin it is! Three causes for the moan

That rises for three children dead and gone!
Be kind, O King, unto this two and one!

Inis Fál

Now may we turn aside and dry our tears!
And comfort us! And lay aside our fears,
For all is gone!

All comely quality!
All gentleness and hospitality!
All courtesy and merriment

Is gone!
Our virtues, all, are withered every one!
Our music vanished, and our skill to sing!

Now may we quiet us and quit our moan!
Nothing is whole that could be broke! No thing
Remains to us of all that was our own.

The Wave of Cliona

My heart is withered and my health is gone,
For they, who were not easy put upon,
Masters of mirth, and of fair clemency,
Masters of wealth, and gentle charity,
They are all gone!

Mac Carthy Mor is dead,
Mac Carthy of the Lee is finishéd,
Mac Carthy of Kanturk joined clay to clay,
And gat him gone, and bides as deep as they!

Their years, their gentle deeds, their flags are furled!
And deeply down, under the stiffened world,
In chests of oaken wood are princes thrust,
To crumble, day by day, into the dust
A mouth might puff at! Nor is left a trace
Of those who did of grace all that was grace!

O Wave of Cliona, cease thy bellowing!
And let mine ears forget a while to ring
At thy long, lamentable, misery!
The great are dead indeed! The great are dead!
And I, in little time, will stoop my head
And put it under, and will be forgot
With them, and be with them, and, thus, be not!

Ease thee! Cease thy long keening! Cry no more!
End is! And here is end! And end is sore!
And to all lamentation be there end!

If I might come on thee, O howling friend!
Knowing that sails were drumming on the sea
Westward to Eire, and that help would be
Trampling for her upon a Spanish deck,
I'd ram thy lamentation down thy neck.

The Land of Fál

IF poesy have truth at all,
And if a Lion of the Gael
Shall rule the Lovely Land of Fál!
O yellow mast!
O roaring sail!
Carry this letter o'er the sea!
Carry the leadership from me
To great O'Néill.

When You Walk

WHEN you walk in a field,
Look down
Lest you trample
A daisy's crown!

But in a city
Look always high,
And watch
The beautiful clouds go by!

The Street Behind Yours

THE night droops down upon the street,
Shade after shade! A solemn frown
Is pressing to
A deeper hue
The houses drab and brown;
Till all in blackness touch and meet,
Are mixed and melted down.

All is so silent! Not a sound
Comes through the dark! The gas-lamps throw,
From here and there,
A feeble glare
On the pavement cracked below;
On the greasy, muddy ground;
On the houses in a row.

Those rigid houses, black and sour!
Each dark thin building stretching high;
Rank upon rank
Of windows blank
Stare from a sullen eye;
With doleful aspect scowl and glower
At the timid passer-by.

And down between those spectre files
The narrow roadway, thick with mud,
Doth crouch and hide!
While close beside
The gutter churns a flood
Of noisome water through the piles
Of garbage, thick as blood!

And tho' 'tis silent! Tho' no sound
Crawls from the blackness thickly spread!
Yet darkness brings
Grim, noiseless things
That walk as they were dead!
They glide, and peer, and steal around,
With stealthy, silent tread!

You dare not walk! That awful crew
Might speak or laugh as you pass by!
Might touch and paw
With a formless claw,
Or leer from a sodden eye!
Might whisper awful things they knew!
—Or wring their hands and cry!

There is the doorway mean and low!
And there are the houses drab and brown!
And the night's black pall!
And the hours that crawl!
And the forms that peer and frown!
And the lamps' dim flare on the slush below!
And the gutter grumbling down!

To the Four Courts, Please

THE driver rubbed at his nettly chin
With a huge loose forefinger, crooked and black;
And his wobbly violet lips sucked in,
And puffed out again and hung down slack:
A black fang shone through his lop-sided smile,
In his little pouched eye flickered years of guile.

And the horse, poor beast! It was ribbed and forked;
And its ears hung down, and its eyes were old;
And its knees were knuckly; and, as we talked,
It swung the stiff neck that could scarcely hold
Its big skinny head up—then I stepped in,
And the driver climbed to his seat with a grin.

God help the horse, and the driver too!
And the people and beasts who have never a friend!
For the driver easily might have been you,
And the horse be me by a different end!
And nobody knows how their days will cease!
And the poor, when they're old, have little of peace!

A Street

Two narrow files of houses scowl,
Blackened with grime, on either side
Of the road, and through them prowl

Strange men and women, shifty-eyed
And slinking. The drink-shop throws
A flaring yellow light adown

The pavement. The gutter flows
A turbid evil stream. A clown,
Drink-sodden, lurches by and sings

Obscenely. A woman trails behind,
With old bad eyes. Her clothing clings
Rain-soaked about her. No daring wind,

Light-hearted, from a garden blows
The sweetness here of any rose.

Fifty Pounds a Year and a Pension

I HAVE never seen the sun walk in the dawn
On a lawn
While the lark sang, mad with rapture, as he came
Robed in flame
Racing, where the purple mountains' foreheads loom
Through the gloom;

Or noticed him at evening give the sea
His last fee;
Nor the burnished, ruddy, golden, peaceful sheen
Tread the green;
While the wood, with long and longer shadow, bends
As he wends.

And my lips shall never blow an oaten pipe,
Nor the ripe,
Glowing berries crush between them from the brake,
Where they make
Such a picture that the gods might know delight
At the sight!

For I've sat my life away with pen and rule
On a stool;
Totting little lines of figures; and so will,
Tho' the chill

And the languor of grey hairs upon my brow
Mocks me now.

And sometimes while I work I lift my eyes
To the skies;
To the foot or two of heaven which I trace
In the space
That a grimy window grudges to the spot
Where I tot.

And I ask the God who made me and the sun,
What I've done
To be buried in this dark and dreary cave,
As in a grave,
While the world laughs in scorn now and then
At my pen!

But I'll sit and work my utmost and not budge;
Tho' a grudge
Is ever growing in the bosom of a clod
'Gainst the God
Who condemned him in his lifetime to grow fit
For the pit.

What the Tramp Said

WHY should we live when living is a pain?
I have not seen a flower had any scent,
Nor heard a bird sing once! The very rain
Seems dirty! And the clouds, all soiled and rent,
Toil sulkily across the black old sky;
And all the weary stars go moping by;
They care not whither—sea, or mount, or plain,
All's one—and what one gets is never gain!

The sun scowled yesterday a weary while,
That used to beam. The moon last night was grim
With cynic gaze, and frosty sullen smile:
And once I loved to gaze, while, from the rim
Of some great mountain, she would look, and gild
The rustling cornfield. Now she is filled
With bitterness and rancour sour as bile,
And blasts the world's surface every mile.

There is no more sunlight! All the weary world
Is steeped in shadow! And for evermore
The clouds will swarm and press, till I am hurled
Back to the heart of things! Oh, it is sore
And sad and sorry to be living! Let me die
And rest—while all eternity lolls by—
Where the fierce winds of God are closely furled
Ten million miles away from this damned world!

Optimist

I

ALL ye that labour! Every broken man
Bending beneath his load! Each tired heart
That cannot quit its burden! All the clan,
Black-browed and fierce, who feel the smart

Of fortune's lances, wayward, uncontrolled!
All ye who writhe in silence 'neath the sin
That no man knows about! And ye who sold
The freedom of your souls if ye might win

A little ease from strife, and hate the thing
That bought it! Ye who droop, trembling, with pain,
And hunger-haunted, lacking everything
That dignifies existence, and are fain

To lay ye down and die! Hear the behest
—All ye that labour, come to Me, and rest—

II

Let ye be still, ye tortured ones! Nor strive
Where striving's futile! Ye can ne'er attain
To lay your burdens down! All things alive
Must bear the woes of life, and if the pain

Be more than ye can bear, then ye can die!
That is the law! And bootless 'tis to seek
In the deeps of space; beyond the high
Pearl-tinted clouds; out where the moon doth peak

Her silver horns; for all that vastness bows
To Tyrant Toil, and weeps to find
Somewhere an aid. Be ye patient! Rouse
Your shoulders to the load to ye assigned,

And dree your weird! Be sure ye will not moan
Stretched in the narrow bed, beneath the stone!

III

Lo, we are mocked with fancies! And we stretch
Our unavailing arms to anywhere,
Where help is none. The north wind will not fetch
An answer to our cries! Nor on the air,

Fanned by the south wind's van, is friend or aid!
What then is left, but this—That we be brave,
And steadfast in our places! Not afraid
However fell our lot! And we will lave

Us deep in human waters, till the mind
Grows wise and kindly, and we haply steal
A paradise from Nature. Naught can bind
Man closer unto man than that he feel

The trouble of his comrade! So we grope
Through courage, truth, and kindness, back to Hope.

A Bird Sings Now

A BIRD sings now;
Merrily sings he

Of his mate on the bough,
Of her eggs in the tree:

But yonder a hawk
Swings out of the blue,

And the sweet song is finished
—Is this story true?

God now have mercy
On me, and on you!

From Hawk and Kite

Poor fluttered, frightened, silent one!
If we had seen your nest of clay,
We should have passed it, would have gone,
Nor frightened you away.

Are others too must guard a nest
From hawk, and kite, and secret foe,
And that despair is in their breast
Which you this moment know.

Shield the nests where'er they be!
In the house, or in the tree!
Guard the poor from treachery!

What's the Use

WHAT's the use
Of my abuse?

The world will run
Around the sun

As it has done
Since time begun,

When I have drifted
To the deuce;

And what's the use
Of my abuse!

Book VI

THE GOLDEN BIRD

Besides That

If I could get to heaven
By eating all I could,
I'd become a pig,
And I'd gobble up my food!

Or, if I could get to heaven
By climbing up a tree,
I'd become a monkey,
And I'd climb up rapidly!

Or, if I could get to heaven
By any other way
Than the way that's told of,
I'd 'a been there yesterday!

But the way that we are told of
Bars the monkey and the pig!
And is very, very, difficult,
Besides that!

Irony

Thus spake a man in days of old:
I will believe that God can be
The kind, the just, that we are told,
If He will throw down here to me
A bag of gold—

But when his wife rose from her bed
To see what kept her man away,
She found him, with a broken head:
And on the ground beside him lay
. . . A bag of lead!

The Breath of Life

AND while they talked and talked, and while they sat
Changing their base minds into baser coin;
And telling—they! how truth and beauty join,
And how a certain this was good, but that
Was baser than the viper or the toad,
Or the blind beggar glaring down the road;

I turned from them in fury, and I ran
To where the moon shone out upon the height,
Down the long reaches of a summer night
Stretching slim fingers, and the starry clan
Grew thicker than the flowers that we see
Clustered in quiet fields of greenery.

The quietudes that sunder star from star;
The hazy distances of loneliness,
Where never eagle's wing, or timid press
Of lark or wren could venture; and the far
Profundities untroubled and unstirred
By any act of man or thought or word;

These held me with amazement and delight!
I yearned up through the spaces of the sky,
Beyond the rolling clouds, beyond the high
And delicate white moon, and up the height,

And past the rocking stars, and out to where
The aether failed in spaces sharp and bare.

The Breath that is the very Breath of Life
Throbbed close to me! I heard the pulses beat,
That lift the universes into heat!
The slow withdrawal, and the deeper strife
Of His wide respiration—like a sea
It ebbed and flooded through immensity.

The Breath of Life, in wave on mighty wave!
O moon and stars, swell to a raptured song!
Ye mountains, toss the harmony along!
O little men, with little souls to save,
Swing up glad chauntings! Ring the skies above
With boundless gratitude for boundless love!

Probing the ocean to its steepest drop!
Rejoicing in the viper and the toad;
And the blind beggar glaring down the road;
And they, who talk and talk and never stop,
Equally quickening! With a care to bend
The gnat's slant wing into a swifter end.

.   .   .

The silence clung about me like a gift!
The tender night-time folded me around
Protectingly! And, in a peace profound,
The clouds drooped slowly backward, drift on drift
Into the darkness; and the moon was gone;
And soon the stars had vanished, every one.

But on the sky, a hand's-breadth in the west,
A faint cold radiance crept, and soared, and spread;

Until the rustling heavens overhead,
And the grey trees, and grass, were manifest:
Then, through the chill, a golden spear was hurled,
And the great sun tossed laughter on the world!

Barbarians

I PAUSE beside the stream, and hear
The waters talking on the way;
If I had a proper ear
I could tell you what they say!

Yon lovely tree against the sky,
Which the sun first rests upon,
Has a message for my eye;
If I had a proper one!

On the heath I met a wind.
It whispered to me as I stood;
If I had a proper mind
I had surely understood!

I am deaf and dumb and blind!
No reply can I invent
When a stream, a tree, a wind,
Asks am I intelligent!

On a Reed

I HAVE a reed of oaten straw,
I play upon it when I may;
And the music that I draw
Is as happy as the day.

It has seven holes, and I
Play it high, and play it low;
I can make it laugh, or cry,
Can make or banish joy or woe.

Any song that you can name
I will play it on the word;
Old or new is all the same,
I'm as ready as a bird.

But there is a tune, and though
I try to play it, day and night,
Blowing high, and blowing low,
I can never play it right!

I know it well, without a flaw,
The tune that yet I cannot play

On my reed of oaten straw,
Though I practise night and day!

Penny pipe, be good to me!
And play the tune I want to play,
Or I will smash you on a tree,
And throw your wicked halves away!

If I Had Wings Just like a Bird

If I had wings just like a bird
I would not say a single word;
I'd spread my wings, and fly away
Beyond the reach of yesterday!

If I could swim just like a fish
I'd give my little tail a swish;
I'd swim ten days and nights, and then
I never would be found again!

Or, if I were a comet bright,
I'd drop in secret every night
Ten million miles! And no one would
Know where I kept my solitude!

But I am not a bird, or fish,
Or comet; so I need not wish:
And need not try to get away
Beyond the reach of yesterday.

Damn yesterday! And this and that,
And these and those! And all the flat,
Dull catalogue of weighty things
That somehow fasten to my wings!

Over the pine trees, and the mountain top!
Never to stop lifting wide wings!
To fly, and fly, and fly
Into the sky!

The Voice of God

I BENT again unto the ground
And I heard the quiet sound
Which the grasses make when they
Come up laughing from the clay.

—*We are the voice of God!*—they said:
Thereupon I bent my head
Down again that I might see
If they truly spoke to me.

But, around me, everywhere,
Grass and tree and mountain were
Thundering in mighty glee,
—*We are the voice of deity!*—

And I leapt from where I lay:
I danced upon the laughing clay:
And, to the rock that sang beside,
—*We are the voice of God!*—I cried.

The Fulness of Time

On a rusty iron throne,
Past the furthest star of space,
I saw Satan sit alone,
Old and haggard was his face;
For his work was done, and he
Rested in eternity.

And to him from out the sun
Came his father and his friend,
Saying,—Now the work is done
Enmity is at an end—
And He guided Satan to
Paradises that He knew.

Gabriel, without a frown;
Uriel, without a spear;
Raphael, came singing down,
Welcoming their ancient peer;
And they seated him beside
One who had been crucified!

Hate

My enemy came nigh;
And I
Stared fiercely in his face:
My lips went writhing back in a grimace,
And stern I watched him from a narrowed eye:

Then, as I turned away,
My enemy,
That bitter-heart, and savage, said to me:

—Some day, when this is past;
When all the arrows that we have are cast;
We may ask one another why we hate,
And fail to find a story to relate:
It may seem to us, then, a mystery
That we could hate each other—
Thus said he; and did not turn away;
Waiting to hear what I might have to say!

But I fled quickly: fearing, if I stayed,
I might have kissed him, as I would a maid.

Soft Wings

I SAW a beggar woman bare
Her bosom to the winter air,
And into the tender nest
Of her famished mother-breast
She laid her child;
And him beguiled,
With crooning song, into his rest.

With crooning song, and tender word,
About a little singing bird,
That spread soft wings about her brood!
And tore her bosom for their food!
And sang the while,
Them to beguile,
All in the forest's solitude!

And, hearing this, I could not see
That she was clad in misery!
For in her heart there was a glow
Warmed her bare feet in the snow!
In her heart was hid a sun
Would warm a world for every one!

In Waste Places

As a naked man I go
Through the desert, sore afraid;
Holding high my head, although
I'm as frightened as a maid.

The lion crouches there! I saw
In barren rocks his amber eye!
He parts the cactus with his paw!
He stares at me, as I go by!

He would pad upon my trace
If he thought I was afraid!
If he knew my hardy face
Veils the terrors of a maid.

He rises in the night-time, and
He stretches forth! He snuffs the air!
He roars! He leaps along the sand!
He creeps! He watches everywhere!

His burning eyes, his eyes of bale
Through the darkness I can see!
He lashes fiercely with his tail!
He makes again to spring at me!

I am the lion, and his lair!
I am the fear that frightens me!
I am the desert of despair!
And the night of agony!

Night or day, whate'er befall,
I must walk that desert land,
Until I dare my fear, and call
The lion out to lick my hand!

The Golden Bird

If Joy, the Golden Bird, would fly,
Do not close an hand upon her!
She belongeth to the sky,
With all the winds of heaven on her:
Only when her wings are free
Bird of Lovely Life is she.

He who Joy of Life would store,
Heart of his be widely open;
Throw the key out with the door,
Throw the hope out with the hopen:
Give her—as she finds in sky—
Place to dip, and soar, and fly.

She will come again, I wist!
She of thee shall not be frighted!
She shall sing upon thy fist!
By her shall thy dark be lighted!
By her freedom thou art given
Right and room in joyous heaven!

The Tale of Mad Brigid

AND then
There rung a bell
Out of the evening air:
One big star fell
In a long golden flare
Through a great stillness,
And He was standing there.

There came a chillness
Creeping through me slow,
Nor could I know
That it was truly He
Who stood beside,
When, lo!
He smiled,
And I was made to know;
Nor hesitate
Because of His grave kingliness and state,
And steady eyes, and brows immaculate.

But then the weight
Of His too sudden glory bowed me down
Slow to the ground:
I feared that He might frown

Without a sound!
Or speak in fire!

Then He said "Sweet!"
And I was dumb;
I dared not come
Because of my desire:
And He went slow away—

And, from the grey
Cold evening,
Came the "tweet"
—Sad to my heart,
But infinitely sweet—
Of some late-flying wren.

The Rose on the Wind

DIP and swing!
Lift and sway!
Dream a life
In a dream, away!

Like a dream
In a sleep
Is the rose
On the wind!

And a fish
In the deep;
And a man
In the mind!

Dreaming to lack
All that is his!
Dreaming to gain
All that he is!

Dreaming a life,
In a dream, away!
Dip and swing!
Lift and sway!

The Merry Music

LETTING the merry music stray
In flirt of leaf, and flirt of wing!
All along a sunny way
Intermits sweet bubbling!
Loveliness is come, and gone,
And scarce was even looked upon!

Golden chime, and silver chime!
Silver laughter, golden joy!
Happy song, not come to rhyme!
Lovely thought, that words annoy!
Comes the dream of living—and
Vanishéd is Fairy-land!

Who has drunk an air that shone,
Or breathed on a note of gold,
Has seen them disappearing on
The lip that took, the lip that told:
While—life danced on in careless way,
Letting the merry music stray!

The Petal of a Rose

LET us be quiet for a while,
The morrow comes! Let us be still!
Let us close our eyes and smile,
Knowing that the morrow will

Come as certain as the sun
Or a sorrow! Let us be
Peaceful till this night be done!
And we rise again to see

That the thing is not in view!
That the memory is gone!
That the world is made anew
Different for every one!

Different! The morrow glows
Where the black wings spread and brood,
Where the petal of a rose
Blushes in the solitude!

Arpeggio

HE wills to be
Alone,
With thee!

A stone,
A stream,
A sky,
A tree!

It is
His
Dream
—To be

Alone,
With these,
And thee!

No More of Woeful Misery I Sing

No more of woeful Misery I sing!
Let her go mope adown the pavèd way!
While to the sunny fields, to everything
That laughs, and to the birds that sing,
I pass along and tune my happy lay!
O sunny sky!
O meadows that the happy clouds are drifting by!

I go at ease by the easy-sliding stream
As by a friend! I dance in solitude
Among the trees! Or lie and gaze and dream
Along the grass! Or hearken to the theme
A lark discourses to her tender brood!
O sunny sky!
O meadows that the happy clouds are drifting by!

There is a thrush lives snugly in a wall;
She lets me peep, unfeared, into her nest;
She lets me see and touch the speckled ball
Under her wing; and does not fear at all,
Although her shy companion is distressed:
O sunny sky!
O meadows that the happy clouds are drifting by!

Sing yet, sing once again, ye birds of joy!
Tell out from branch and bough the endless tale
Of happiness, that nothing can annoy;
What if your mates seem timorous and coy,
If ye sing high enough how can ye fail?
O sunny sky!
O meadows that the happy clouds are drifting by!

On every side, far as the eye can see,
The round horizon, like a bosom's swell,
Seems brooding in a sweet maternity,
Where no thing may be hurt! Not even me!
But she will stoop and kiss and make us well!
O sunny sky!
O meadows that the happy clouds are drifting by!

I am the brother of each bird, and tree,
And everything that grows—your children glad!
Their hearts are in my heart, their ecstasy!
O Mother of all Mothers, comfort me!
Give me your breast for I am very sad!
O sunny sky!
O meadows that the happy clouds are drifting by!

On a Lonely Spray

UNDER a lonely sky, a lonely tree
Is beautiful! All that is loneliness
Is beautiful! A feather, lost at sea;
A staring owl; a moth; a yellow tress
Of seaweed on a rock, is beautiful!

The night-lit moon, wide-wandering in sky!
A blue-bright spark, where ne'er a cloud is up!
A wing, where no wing is, it is so high!
A bee in winter! And a buttercup,
Late blown! are lonely, and are beautiful!

She whom you saw but once, and saw no more!
That he who startled you, and went away!
The eye that watched you from a cottage door!
The first leaf, and the last! The break of day!
The mouse, the cuckoo, and the cloud, are beautiful!

For all that is, is lonely! All that may
Will be as lonely as is that you see!
The lonely heart sings on a lonely spray!
The lonely soul swings lonely in the sea!
And all that loneliness is beautiful!

All: all alone: and all without a part
Is beautiful! For beauty is all-where!
Where is an eye, is beauty! Where an heart,
Is beauty, breathing out on empty air,
All that is lonely, and is beautiful!

Death

Slow creatures, slow,
Nuzzle and press,
And take their food
In the darkness!

No stir is now
In all that once was all!
No dream; no sound;
No sight; no sense is there!

Unseen, the beam of the sun!
Unknown, the ring of the light!
Unknown, in the cave!
Unseen, by the slow, slow, hungers!

Naught's left
—But food!
All else, that was,
Is away!

—Far away
In the Gleam!
In the Ring!
In the Beam!
In the Sun!

The Crest Jewel

I

THE leaf will wrinkle to decay,
And crumble into dust away!

The rose, the lily, grow to eld,
And are, and are no more, beheld!

Nothing can stay! For, as the eye
Rests upon an object nigh,

It is not there to look upon!
It is mysteriously gone!

And, in its place, another thing
Apes its shape and fashioning!

II

All that the sun will breathe to-day
The moon will lip and wear away

To-night! And all will rebegin
To-morrow as the dawn comes in!

Is no beginning, middle-trend,
Or argument to that, or end!

No cause and no effect, and no
Reason why it should be so!

Or why it might be otherwise
To other minds, or other eyes!

III

The soul can dream itself to be
Adrift upon an endless sea

Of day and night! The soul can seem
To be all things that it can dream!

And yet may look within to find
That which is steady in the wind!

That which the fire does not appal!
Which good and ill move not at all!

Which does not seek, or lack, or try!
And was not born, and cannot die!

IV

It has been writ in wisdom old—
This is the last word to be told:

—There is no dissolution! No
Creation! There are none in woe!

There is no teacher, teaching, taught!
Are none who long for, lack for aught!

Are none who pine for freedom! None
Are liberated under sun!

—And this is absolutely true
In Him who dreams in me and you.

Thy Soul

YOUNG Nachiketas went to Death!
He bargained with the Monarch grim
For Knowledge, as the Katha saith,
And Death revealed the Soul to him!
And who learns with the fearless lad
Hath All that Nachiketas had.

Death said:—

From That the sun and moon arise;
They set in That again:
From That are seas, and stars, and skies,
And trees, and beasts, and men:
And That of Soul is This of Sense;
Between Them is no difference.

All that is Here, the same is There;
All that is There is Here:
There is no difference Anywhere;
The One doth All appear!
From death to death he goes, who sees
Differences, or Degrees.

That which is told of, That Thou Art,
There is no other Sprite;

No heaven, nor earth, nor middle part,
There is no day, or night;
There is no beauty, truth, or wit,
But That alone! And Thou Art It!

He dreameth—I am moon, and sun;
I am the earth, and sea;
I am the strife, the lost, the won;
I am Variety—
He dreameth This, and That, and Thou,
In past, and future time, and now!

He is the Dreamer, and the Dream!
He is the Frightened, and the Fear!
He is the Hope! the Gloom! the Gleam!
He is the Season, and the Year!
—He is not This, nor That, nor Yon:
He is Thyself! And Thou Art One!

He will not be obtained by speech;
Not by the mind, the ear, the eye;
He cometh, in His time, to each
Who Him affirm, courageously:
Thou Art! He Is! And that is all
That may be told, or can befall!

Fast not, nor pray! But only know,
He Is—I am—And all is done!
The Deed of Time is finished! Lo,
Thy Self to Thine own Self art won!
Thou shalt not seek, nor have, reply,
For Thou Art That, in blink of eye.

Thou knew it all! 'Twas hid within
Thy Memory! Call but to mind
This, that Thou Art, and Death nor Sin

Shall conquer Thee again! Nor bind
Thine action! Nor make Thee to seem
A Dreamer, living in a Dream!

Awake!
Arise!
Put glory on,
Of which all Soul and Sense is wrought!
Thou shalt be naught Thou dreamed upon
Of good or evil Thing! Nor aught
That thought doth bicker at!
Thou shalt be Naught!
And Thou shalt be
Thy Self, and Thine own Mystery!
Knowledge! Bliss! Eternity!
For Thou Art That!

The Pit of Bliss

1

WHEN I was young
I dared to sing
Of everything,
And anything!
Of Joy, and woe, and fate, and God!
Of dreaming cloud, and teeming sod!
Of hill that thrust an amber spear
Into the sunset! And the sheer
Precipice that shakes the soul
To its black gape—I sang the whole
Of God and Man, nor sought to know
Man or God, or Joy, or Woe!
And, though an older wight I be,
My soul hath still such Ecstasy
That, on a pulse, I sing and sing
Of Everything, and Anything!

2

There is a Light
Shines in the head:
It is not gold,
It is not red,

But, as the lightning's blinding light,
It is a stare of silver white
That one surmise might fancy blue!
On that, mind-blinding, hue I gaze
An instant, and am in a maze
Of thinking—could one call it so?
It is no thinking that I know!
—An hurricane of Knowing, that
Could whelm the soul that was not pat
To flinch, and lose the deadly thing;
—And Sing, and Sing again, and Sing
Of Everything, and Anything!

3

An Eagle
Whirling up the sky;
Sunblind! Dizzy!
Urging high,
And higher beating yet a wing,
Until he can no longer cling,
Or hold; or do a thing, but fall,
And sink, and whirl, and scream, through all
His dizzy, heaven-hell of Pit,
In mile-a-minute flight from It
That he had dared! From height of height,
So the Poet takes his flight
And tumble in the Pit of Bliss!
And, in the roar of that Abyss,
And falling, he will Sing and Sing
Of Everything, and Anything!

4

What is Knowing?
'Tis to see!
What is Feeling?

'Tis to be!
What is Love? But, more and more,
To See and Be! To be a Pour
And Avalanche of Being, till
Being ceases, and is still
For very motion—What is Joy?
—Being, past all earthly cloy
And intermixture! Being spun
Of Itself is Being won!
That is Joy—And this is God,
To be That, in cloud and clod:
And, in cloud, and clod, to Sing
Of Everything, and Anything!

Book VII

STRICT JOY

Sarasvati

As bird to nest, when, moodily,
The storm-cloud murmurs nigh the tree,
Thus let him flee,
Who can to sing,
Here hath he calm, and sheltering.

As bee to hive, when, with the sun,
Long honey-gathering is done,
Who can to sing,
There let him flee,
This is his cell, his companie.

As child to mother running, where
The thunder shudders through the air,
Thus let him flee,
Who can to sing,
Here hath he ward, and cherishing.

Fly to thy talent! To thy charm!
Thy nest, thine hive, thy sheltering arm!
Who can to sing,
There let him flee,
This is, naught else is, certainty.

Demiurge

1

WISE Emotion, some have thought,
Is that whereby a poem's wrought:
More will have it, that the Hive
The Bee comes from, and all alive,

Is Thought: while others fret to tell,
Imagination, like a well,
Bubbles all that is to be
Into shape and certainty.

2

Imagination does but seem:
Thought is wisdom, in a dream:
And Emotion can, with strain,
Tell a pleasure from a pain:

These, the Sleepy Ones and Dull,
That nothing sow, and nothing cull,
Nothing have that's fit to sing
The Wide-Awake, the Living Thing.

3

The living, ever-waking Will:
The ever-spacious, ever-still:
Wherefrom, as from a fountain, springs
All that praises, soars, and sings:

All that is not dull and dense,
Bogged in thought, and clogged in sense,
Comes unbid, and surge on surge,
From the Will, the Demiurge.

Cadence

SEE the lightning
Leaping in the sky
How fleet he goes:

See the rose
Leaping to the eye
How neat she blows:

See the mother
Running to her child
How sweet she goes!

Strict Care, Strict Joy!

TO W. T. H. HOWE

I

To-DAY I felt as poor O'Brien did
When, turning from all else that was not his,
He took himself to that which was his own
—He took him to his verse—for other all
He had not, and (tho' man will crave and seek)
Another all than this he did not need.

So, pen in hand, he tried to tell the whole
Tale of his woe in rhyming; lodge the full
Weight of his grief in versing: and so did:
Then—when his poem had been conned and cared,
And all put in that should not be left out—
Did he not find, and with astonishment,

That grief had been translated, or was come
Other and better than it first looked to be:
And that this happed, because all things transfer
From what they seem to that they truly are
When they are innocently brooded on
—And, so, the poet makes grief beautiful.

2

"Behold me now, with my back to the wall,
Playing music to empty pockets!"
So, Raftery, tuning a blind man's plight,
Could sing the cark of misery away;
And know, in blindness and in poverty,
That woe was not of him, nor kin to him.

And Egan Rahilly begins a verse—
"My heart is broken, and my mind is sad . . ."
'Twas surely true when he began his song,
And was less true when he had finished it:
—Be sure, his heart was buoyant, and his grief
Drummed and trumpeted as grief was sung!

For, as he meditated misery
And cared it into song—strict care, strict joy!
Caring for grief he cared his grief away:
And those sad songs, tho' woe be all the theme,
Do not make us to grieve who read them now
—Because the poet makes grief beautiful.

3

And I, myself, conning a lonely heart
—Full lonely 'twas, and 'tis as lonely now—
Turned me, by proper, to my natural,
And, now, too long her vagrant, wooed my Muse:
Then to her—Let us look more close to these,
And, seeing, know; and, knowing, be at ease.

Seeing the sky o'ercast, and that the rain
Had plashed the window, and would plash again:
Seeing the summer lost, and winter nigh:

Seeing inapt, and sad, and fallen from good:
Seeing how will was weak, and wish o'er-bearing:
Seeing inconstant: seeing timidity:

Seeing too small, too poor, in this and yon:
Seeing life, daily, grow more difficult:
Seeing all that moves away—moving away
. . . And that all seeing is a blind-man's treat,
And that all getting is a beggar's dole,
And that all having is a bankruptcy . . .

4

All these, sad all! I told to my good friend,
Told Raftery, O'Brien, Rahilly,
Told rain, and frosted blossom, and the summer gone,
Told poets dead, and captains dead, and kings!
—And we cared naught that these were mournful things,
For, caring them, we made them beautiful.

Apple Blossom

1

HE thought
Of naught
But the Blossom of the Apple:

He thought:
—Than aught
That blows on tree

Sweetest is that sweet blossom
—And sweeter than that
Is she—

2

Now he is mad,
And naught's to do
—How could he other be, who had

These twelve
Long months
Thus brooded you,

And thought
Of naught
But the Blossom of the Apple!

The White Swan

COULD you but see her
—She would seem
Like some bright star
That is seen in dream:
Like a sun-burst
Seen on a wintry day
When all, but one bright spot,
Is grey.

Could you but see her
—That would be
As when one sees
On a flooding sea
The white foam ride;
Or sees a proud swan,
Buoyantly,
Breasting a tide.

In Memoriam

1

BEHIND the barrack wall, at break of day:
Where night died slow, and day delayed to come:
Where winter brooded in a cloud of grey,
And life was unawake, and bleak and numb:

Where loneliness looked out on lonely air,
All chill and utter loneliness among:
Where sight and sound were muffled, and despair
Alone had tingling finger-tip and tongue!

2

The patience born of pride and gentleness,
They saw, who stared you down that wintry day,
—The last look you should see, and pitiless!
Ere sight and sound were shattered all away,

And unthanked worth was drowned in bloody dew
—Now endless love hath ending, and is done:
Now duty, service, torment, ends for you:
And you may take the rest that you have won.

256

3

Where no dream burrows in the silent clay
Of tireless insult! Where the patient mole,
Ingratitude, that eateth life away,
Comes not, nor nibbles nigh—sleep there, good soul!

.   .   .

And now with store of pale and wintered gold,
The sun shall wake the town, and gild the spire;
Shall brighten all dull waters, and infold
All that is grey, all that is gloom in fire;
Shall chide and mend despair, and hearten hope
To dream again the Land of Heart's Desire.

Reverie on a Rose

HE is there,
And she is there,
And I am here:

I think it clear
He should be here
When I am here.

   .   .   .

But he is there,
And I am here
—And she is fair—

(Not that I fear
That would be queer!
But he is there!)

   .   .   .

I sitting here:
She sitting there:
—The rose I wear

(His rose) I tear
And drop it here,
For he is there!

   .   .   .

If I am dear
He should be here
When I am here!

But he is there!
I do not care
—Let him stop there!

THEME AND VARIATIONS

TO STEPHEN MAC KENNA

Introduction

LET the poet pluck a reed,
A lazy, a luxuriant weed

And sing for singing! Pens are such,
They write too little, or too much,
And smudge a somewhat all they touch!

Thus to begin it—That I got
The book you sent, and that I'm not
Adequate at all, nor fit
For half one half of half of it.

So, when great Plotinus came
He found me playing at my game,
Moving the will, the mind, the pen,
To moods that lie beyond the ken
Of poet or
Philosopher.

Theme

THE golden eve is all astir,
And tides of sunset flood on us
—Incredible, miraculous—
We look with adoration on
Beauty coming, beauty gone,
That waits not any looking on.

Thoughts will bubble up, and break,
Spilling a sea, a limpid lake,
Into the soul; and, as they go
—Lightning visitors! we know
A lattice opened, and the mind
Poised for all that is behind
The lattice, and the poising mind.

Could the memory but hold!
—All the sunsets, flushed with gold,
Are streaming in it!

All the store
Of all that ever was before
Is teeming in it!

All the wit
Of holy living, holy writ,
Waiting till we remember it,
Is dreaming in it!

Variations

1

WITHIN a dream lies trapped a doubt!
That lets not go: this dares not out;
Lest worse of utter blank enwrap,
In unimaginable trap,
Desire—the web and mesh of dream—
And Mind—that hath for only theme
To doubt, desire, despair, and be
Ignorance, inconstancy!

Creator in creation strayed!
The Knower frightened at a name!
The Maker lost in what is made!
The Player played on by the game!
In immanence the Immanent,
—Through all dispers'd, extended, spread—
Is caught, and in imprisonment
In all that He imaginéd!

2

Only the Universal Mind,
Our Stay, and Star, and Diadem,
Can touch to sight all that is blind,
And with Its light illumine them
That lack for light.

By grace of It, by heavenly chance,
The slow, the loath, the idle Will

May pierce forgetfulness, and still
Desire—that whole of ignorance!
And bring all back to memory.

The Truth, the Self of all Thou art!
Sole Being! Sole Reality!
Be Heart's Desire in every heart!
Be All in All! And be increase
To all of Bliss, and Power, and Peace!

3

Courage and Hope art Thou,
And Loveliness:

Bid all we have of fear
To fear no more:

And urge all hope
That it may hope for all:

And tell all love
That all it loves is lovely.

4

An eye, an ear, a sense of touch!
—Are we not gifted quite as much
As cats and dogs are? Shall we not
Get everything that can be got
By eye and ear, that get and store
All that they give, and nothing more?

They give that lazy imbecile
—The mind—a sight, a sound, a feel:
And he resolves, with wisdom fit,
That It is That, and That is It:

Nor wots that It and That and Us
Are utterly not these, nor thus.

They understate, disguise and cheat:
Their lightning, like the slug, is fleet:
Their thunder whispers matter for
Inclusion in a metaphor:
And life's a noun, which they will give
In marriage to an adjective.

The Good, the Beautiful, the True,
The Never-Old, the Ever-New,
The All-Unique. . . . What should they do,
But look and listen? Till they find
—Seeing, hearing, and the mind—
That Mystery of Mysteries
Is dumb and dark to such as these.

5

That every eye
Is looked through by
I Am:

That every cry
Is uttered by
I Am:

That every why
Is answered by
I Am!

6

Come, all ye friends, be of good cheer!
There is an end to every day:

There is an end to every year:
The centuries shall wear away:

The hills shall crumble down, and roll
Underneath an iron sea:
And the tropics with the pole
Shall be frozen equally:

Let Adam's son strike on the lyre
And be content, for he shall seem
Untouched by all that is desire,
Unreached by all that is a dream!

7

He loves the sun:
But in the white
Light of the moon
He knows delight
That day is done.

Too much, too oft, too many, he
Has seen, and been, and borne, to stay
Slave of the Light one moment more
Who, with one wish, may wish away
This outflung All:

Recall, dismiss, and exorcise
The hand, the mind, the seen, the seer
—All that is ignorant or wise
Annihilating, with a stark
Let there be Dark!

8

The small, green leaf
Fell down from the tree:

And the great oak tree
Fell down from the cliff:

And the huge, hard cliff
Slipped down to the sea:

And the sea was sucked
To the sun in a whiff:

Then . . . blink!
And a shout!

And the sun
Blew out . . .

9

No bees, no leaves:
No carollings sung:
No linnets in the eaves,
No young!

Ice, deep in the dale:
Ice, thick in the wold:
Ice, white in the vale:
Ice-cold!

Ice, trapped in ice!
—Oh foolish fear!
For the south blows spice,
And the rose is seen,

And the lark
Is here,
And the woods
Are green!

10

Look you, the fly, come to the spider's web,
Quick-clutched is, parcelled is, and is devoured!
And the gay bird—that, over the woodland wild,
Shrills out what ecstasy—snaps spider up!
Whom, ere one note again he can, the cat,
Quick-quiet, taketh—when, in similar,
Vain, and in vain, forth from the grim, grey dog
That followeth close, and close, and lets not ever,
Vainly she flies—nor flies not far, nor long,
Ere down, she too . . . and he, and all that is,
Soon felled, goes murdered down—Eater and eaten,
Murdered and murderer, goes murdering down.

11

Strange frenzy, wakening at heart of love!
O cruelty, at mid of gentleness!
Horror, at quick and very pith of life!
From that, from such, of ill, unreasoning,
How shall we see! How dwell upon! Or out
To credible bring what from imbecile!

Murdered and murdering! Though love be law,
And nature's self hath licence but of it!
If she but call, all these, unhesitant,
Unreckoning, unstayed—and, with them, we—
Forthright, appalled, to quittance, and to doom,
Hasty, and terrified, and hopeless, go!

12

Speed, skill, nor courage; goodness, wisdom, beauty,
May not retard, refuse it, nor avoid!
In one same terror, and in common ruin,
Strait, to the darkling blank, and grim abrupt,

These all—our known, mode of our life—and we,
Murdered and murdering, go hasty down!

Into not-known, into vacuity!
Into unbottomed dreadful, and a dark!
Where life saith—No, I go not—and is gone!
Where naught is but which would, and utter cannot!
Where, in black blank and null, the wary ghost
Hearkens, nor hears; and, with no voice, would wail!

13

Fear is, where is no cause!
To this, all-dark,
The small child comes
A-wearying of the day:
And the bird
—Sight-tired, light-weary, sun-sick—
Seeks here his sleep at dark'ning evenfall:
Glad to relinquish space and aery-light:
Glad to forget—and to forget he can!
The too-seen, and the too-known,
In the better-known,
In the first-known,
In the deep-dark!

14

From dream of dark to dream of light,
From dream of naught to dream of all,
He goes, nor aught relinquisheth,
Dreaming a dream perpetual.

He hath his mood and fancying;
And now he would, and now would not:
And bids his sun be took away:
And bids his darkness be forgot!

And bids his light and dark not be:
And bids his known to be unknown:
And bids nor unbids more, for he
Is All, and is Himself alone!

15

There is no pain, nor aught that worketh it:
Is no despair, nor what may be despaired:
Not one that feareth death, nor suffereth it:
Doubt and despair and misery and death,
This is thy mind at play: this is thy mind,
Creator, that wills and doubts and wonders!
He saith—Do not believe it! Do not hold
As seen one scene it showeth, nor as done
One deed it seemeth forth! From dim recalled
To mirage realised! Of nothing made,
Of nothing capable! 'Tis but a dream
In vacancy, dreamed by the conjurer.

16

The wing that bears the albatross
Over the gulf that he would cross
Is kingly: royal, too, the eye
Staring the utter deep and high,
The void and monstrous steep of sky:

Breasting on desolation rude:
Beating a van in solitude:
Not dizzying on't, nor wondering
If that which bears aloft the wing
May fail the wing!

17

He dares to be alone! He dares
Waste, and blank, and mystery:

Not desolation, dreadful airs,
Not silence, nor the clamouring sea
Can edge his wise tranquillity,
Nor fret his joy—
                    For only this,
To be sufficient and alone,
Is joy, and joy's rewarding kiss,
Is ecstasy, and all of bliss
That bird, or man, or god hath known.

18

In dreadful airs, and frightful sky,
As watchful, unafraid, serene,
They fly who dare, and will, to fly,
The utter deep, the matchless high,
Poising a gulf is not terrene:

So tenuous, so sparest-thin,
So only for the spirit fit,
Rarer than thought dare venture in,
That loath to it, and lead to it,
Imagination baulks at it!

19

On wing more tense than ever stirred
The albatross, the kingly bird,
Serene, and joyous, and aware,
Into the blank of Everywhere,
Or Knowledge, do these Great repair!

Finding, unhid, the magic rod
That charms the brute into the god:
Raising the living from the dead,
Drawing, as from reluctant lead,
The gold of being, godlihead!

Seeking the sword, the shoes, the cape,
That saves us from our angry ape,
The Mind—the Monster in the Stream,
The Mind—the Ignorance Supreme,
That holds the Doubter in the Dream!

20

All comes and goes,
The rose
Blossoms and fades away:

Grey leaps to gold,
And gold
Sleeps into grey:

And all that leaped
From clay
Is steeped in clay!

. . .

—But He,
The Self,
The Watcher of the Race,

The One,
The Witness,
Knower of the Plot,

Who bears life
As a mask
Upon a face,

He goeth not!

21

Nothing is easy! Pity then
The poet more than other men:

And, since his aim is ecstasy,
And, since none work so hard as he,
Forgive the poet poesy!

He hath the same dull eyes: his ears
Are dull-attuned: his hopes and fears
Are those same ravening dogs that bay
The moon, and bury bones in clay!

Tho' he on offals, too, was bred,
Tho' in his heart, and in his head,
The brute doth slaver, yet he can
Banish the brute from off the man,
The man from that beyond the man.

He gave a song, a wing, to words
That they might fly and sing like birds
In love, who cannot too much sing
The heaven, the earth, the everything;
And love, the air that buoys along
The wing, the singer, and the song.

Yea, wonder is that he hath done,
For all that is beneath the sun
By magic he transfigures to
A better sound, a finer view:
And—loveliest tale of all that's true!
He tells that you come to the spring,
And that the spring returns to you.

22

Bush calling to bush
As sister to brother,
   Telling of spring:

The cuckoo, the thrush
Reply to each other,
   All in the spring:

And, deep in the sweet
Green heart of the wood
   —Glory of spring:

The throstle will whistle
And tend to his brood,
   Singing the spring!

23

The spring,
And He,
The Watcher of the Race!

The One,
The Witness,
Knower of the Plot!

Who bears life
As a mask
Upon a face,

He goeth not!

Coda

I GIVE you thanks and love, as due
To all of truth that is as true
As you, good friend, and best of men
That was, is, or may be again.

Yet did I lip one half the lay
That half-expressed one half I'd say
To you, of you—'twould be a lore
Was never piped by reed before.

But, well you know it, reeds are such,
They pipe too little, or too much,
Transposing music to a key
Was not, is not, and should not be

. . . And here I end my melody!

Book VIII

KINGS AND THE MOON

I Am Writer

I AM writer,
And do know
Nothing that is false,
Or true:

Have only care
To take it so,
And make it sing,
And make it new:

And make it new,
And make it sing,
When, if it's pleasing
Unto you,

Say, I've done
A useful thing
—As your servant
Ought to do.

In the Red

WHEN I was young
I had no sense
—Now I'm older
None have I:

I had no fiddle,
Had no pence
—Now I'm older
None have I:

There was no tune
That I could play
—Now I'm older
None play I:

But, over the hills,
And far away!
—Now I'm older
There am I.

To Lar, with a Biscuit

THERE is no more
An Household God:
The Presiding Deities
Are gone,
Are sacked.

Love was all
They had for rod:
Not-loving all
They knew of wrong,
And thwacked.

No watch
Is on the household now!
Penates, Lares,
Emigrate,
Begone!

Daughters, sons,
Do anyhow:
And, as you please,
Perpetuate,
Each one,

279

The skunk, the badger,
And the cow!
—No altar's
In the household now,
No wit—

Only the monkey
And the sow
Tell what man should do,
And how
Do it.

Envying Tobias

No more do we
Of angels talk:
'Tis no more of any read

That an angel came
With us to walk,
And to a woman said

—Blessed be thou,
To thee I bow
My wise and lovely head—

.   .   .

I need an angel,
Such as young
Tobias met:

Now do, to me,
God, my dear,
Send quickly here

That angel, which shall be
Teacher to Thine own every son,
And bring this son to Thee.

Paternoster

Do never pray,
But only say
—O Thou!

And leave it so,
For He will know,
—Somehow—

That you fall,
And that you call
On Him now.

Student Taper

WHEN,
—At the mid of moon,
At end of day—
My lamp is lit,
Grant me a boon,
I pray,
And do
So order it

—That the small creatures,
Terrified and blind:
The gold and silvern moths
Of lovely kind,
Do not whirl to my taper,
Nor, therein,
Die, painfully,
And bring my light
To sin.

My light
Is innocent!
Grant
—That it may be
Harmless,
And helpful,
And remarked
Of Thee.

Te Deum

In terror,
Planning evasion
—All-calm in terror!

Fearful and eager,
—Inventing obstruction—
As eager as fearful!

Cowering, and scurrying,
The old rat,
—Shivering in the barn,

Crouching
From the dog's mouth
To the dark corner—

All-watchful
Has seen escape,
All-striving,

Is free!

Shall He—Wilt Thou?

SHALL my dog praise me!
—Let him love instead—
Beloved then is he,
And cherishéd.

Wilt thou praise God!
—Do not so foolishly—
Mere love, and so shall He,
And cherish thee.

Gathering the Waters

I HAVE wasted
Precious time!
—Seeking
What is nowhere found—
Seeking reason,
And to climb
By that to another ground:

I do seek
The cheat no more
—That half-deaf,
And wholly-blind—
Moon,
That was so loved before,
Beam again
Within my mind.

Like a tin-can
In the sun
Reason is:
And, when you get it,
Nothing's got,
And nothing's done,
It will cheat you,
An you let it:

I no more
Do cherish thee
—Tricky, stupid,
Deaf, and blind—
Moon,
That is all-ecstasy,
Beam again
Within my mind.

Thine effulgence
Hath no scheme:
It is innocence
Of light:
Lovely
As an angel's dream
In the mid
And grim of night:

From that other
Let's away
—Pompous, silly—
Dull, and blind—
Moon,
That is all love, alway,
Beam again
Within my mind

Aiding,
With secret beam
And gend'ring influence:
Urging
—In what obscure,
At what remove—
The bud, the blossom, and the fruit,
The all-reluctant

Moves by thee,
And knows of joy.

O moon,
Gentle with blessings!
Of lovely
Loveliest One!
Who sings thee not
Of poesy
Is beggared:
Who loves thee not
Of love
Hath utter none!

Come,
Silverly!
Come,
Gathering the waters,
Gathering the apples!
Mother of all that quickens,
Beam in my dark!
Enter this all-obscure,
And quicken it.

          .   .   .

The moon hath not got any light!
All that beauty, all that power
Is a cheat upon the sight,
Is come and gone within the hour:

What is pure, or what is lovely?
Nothing is that will endure!

An apple-blossom in the spring
—When spring awakens everything—

Is pure or lovely as it please,
Or not, as it knows not of these:

What is pure, or what is lovely?
Nothing is that will endure!

Pure is cherished in a dream,
Loveliness in little thought:
Out of nowhere do they gleam,
Out of nothing are they wrought:

What is pure, or what is lovely?
Nothing is that will endure!

Courage, goodness, tenderness:
Wisdom, beauty, ecstasy:
Wonder, love, and loveliness:
Hope, and immortality:

What is pure, or what is lovely?
Nothing is that will endure!

Pure and lovely sleep and wait
—Where not good nor ill is done—
In the keep, within the gate,
At the heart of everyone:

All is pure, and all is lovely:
All is so, and doth endure.

Bidding the Moon

WHO is not glad
To look on gold,
Or can be sad
In lovely green!

In blue, anew,
The heart
Takes thought,
And thought is told in every part:

In purple
All of kingliness is seen,
And who sees such
Is lover to a queen:

Who seeth red
He seeth manifold,
And manifold is tolled
Within his head.

Rejoice in all that's seen,
Or said,
The gold, the green,
The purple, and the red.

       .   .   .

Look you on blind as love,
On black as night,
And see
All that has cared for thee,
In black look to all light:

This bids the moon to rise,
Brings rest
To all that sees:
Brings bird to nest,
And eyes
To skies,
And all souls to their knees:
And God and Love,
Brings Love and God
To the cherishing of these.

KINGS AND TANISTS

Coronation

THERE is that lion
With the face of a woman,
That horse
With the face of a man:

Lion and horse
—So apart from the human—
Remember,
If memory can,

Some man did give you
The face of a woman,
Some woman
The face of a man:

And were proud,
And were moved,
To be maned,
And be hooved,

And admitted you
Chiefs of their clann.

2

King with Herald

ALL you have gathered,
And have held as gain
—The good,
The beautiful,
The true—
All that was learned
In diligence, and pain,
And taught, in trust, to you,
Dismiss
All this,
For this is worthless all,
And hath no act,
And cometh not to call.

Now welcome Doubt,
Who searcheth all things out,
And questions everything:
Best friend of truth,
And Herald of the King,
And who will not be passed
Of anything:
Who saith
To birth and death
—Whence come you?
What are you?

Urge the loath mind upon all-vacancy:
And, as a tree grows

—Not without thoughtfulness,
But knowing as it knows—
Do you,
From toughest wood
And heavenly dew,
Grow blossoms of all good:
The seed was kind,
Good shall the fruiting be
Of the wise mind,
And of the apple tree.

3

What King

Pass from all this, and know
—That holiness is empty,
Good a word,
Power but a cheating,
And that wisdom is
Impertinence,
And is
Vulgarity.

What thought is worthy of what power?
There is no thought but will decay:
As milk stood in the sun an hour
So will this rot,
And be as not,
And pass away:
Without a trace,
Without a deed,
—This is the withering of the weed!

Win, so,
To poverty,

And be forgot
Of high and low:
Be, even of the gods, remembered not:
Be in no reckoning, not e'en your own:
Now are you rich,
Who now are all alone:
To be alone is wisdom,
To be poor is purity,
To nothing know of these,
Divinity!

And when
—As from afar
Star calls to star—
One calls to thee,
Demanding who you are,
And your degree,
Saying
—Here reigns what king?
To such an one reply
—Here Loneliness doth reign,
That king am I!

4

God Save the King

EVERY now and then
I do wish to be
—More than other men—
All humility:

I do wish to seem
—More than others be—

The dreamer in his dream,
Anonymity:

Let who, or what, or why,
Be answered as may be,
I give no reply,
All stupidity:

I wish away all mind,
Only wish to be
Invisible as wind,
Lonely as a tree:

Lonely, and unknown,
—As all that is must be—
The King is on his throne,
All of majesty!

5
Tanist

REMEMBER the spider
Weaving a snare
—And that you did it
Everywhere:

Remember the cat
Tormenting a bird
—And that you did it
In deed and word:

Remember the fool
Frustrating the good

—And that you did it
Whenever you could:

Remember the devil
And treachery
—And that you did it
When you were he:

Remember all ill
That man can know
—And that you did it
When you were so:

And then remember
Not to forget,
—That you did it,
And do it yet.

6

Lullaby with Drums

O STERILE heart,
And sad!
Here there is nothing
To be had
Of life, or art:

There is here
Nothing that is true,
Nothing you need fear,
Nothing you can do,
Not a thing to challenge you!

There is here
Not a thing to challenge you,

Not a thing that you can do,
Not a thing you need to fear,
Nothing that is true:

Here there is nothing
To be had
Of life, or art,
O sad,
O sterile heart!

7

Do Not

Do not too-greatly chide,
What is thou shalt not void,
Thou shalt abide:
And what
Is not
Who shall provide?

Put thy seed
Into thy clay,

'Twill be fruitful
On a day:

Only this
Fulfils all need,

In thy clay
Plant thy seed.

8

Royally

By night or day,
When praying,
Pray

That you, at last,
May sing,
Or say

—Empty am I
Of everything,
In every way—

.   .   .

Royally,
As crownéd king,
Be glad to die

When you can sing,
Or say,
Or pray

—Of everything,
In every way,
Empty am I.

9

Withdrawn in Gold

LIGHT floods the mind!
And now the mind is pure,

Is naught-intent,
Is empty:

It is withdrawn into its solitude,
—As the moon withdraws,
When storm and rain have blacked the world
        away,
And only the great gold sun rides on the
        main—

The Shining Ones are vanished
In greater splendour,
Withdrawn, not lost, in gold,
In light not gone away:

Stars and the moon
Are lost in the light of life,
As the pure mind, withdrawn,
Is lost in the light of God.

10

Fanfare

SCANNING the forest
On a scarce-moved wing
The kite,
Lord of the air,
Floats, soars,
Goes as he will.

All-uproar
And all-urge,
Crashing
From off a mountain

O'er a sea,
The wind roars wild away.

Seen,
And unseen,
The lightning come
Is gone,
Leaving behind
A herd of thunderings.

. . .

Who will go quickly
Let him be as light:
As that which knows
Not time, nor period:
Which nothing dreams
Of pace, or space, or place.

Quick
As the mind creates,
Preserves,
Destroys,
The light
Is where it is.

This be the norm!
Truly
This speed is his:
He leaves
The lightning lorn,
He is the light!

11

The King

He is come
From wandering the mountain:
From the bleak hills
And craggy solitudes,
Where, in the night,
Is nothing but the moon,
And, in the day,
Only the sun is strong:

Light, without leading!
Beam, without hope, or help:
So is he come
From the moon,
From the sun:
From hope, from doubt, from love, from fear,
He is come
From wandering the mountain.

For the Lion of Judah

TELL what now is happening
On the sole Arabian tree:
There is no song in anything,
No tale of glee,

Since Phoenix and the Dove did part
Love loves no more, no more is kind:
—What is happening in the heart,
What has happened to the mind?

Mind that late did never cease
To hark, to hasten, and to aid,
Bringing comfort, bringing peace
To everything that was afraid!

And the heart that could espy
All that mind can fail to see,
Saying—where naught is am I,
Be not lone, I stay with thee!

   . . .

Here the anthem doth commence,
Here the Swan doth sing the threne,
Pity, Love and Innocence
He remembers to have seen.

—Mind does mind no more, nor care,
Minding is no more its will:
To murder is its main affair,
Treachery its main of skill!

And the heart, that said to Love
—Thou and I—says that no more,
Phoenix and the Turtle-Dove
Show each other to the door.

Only now the third, the wise,
On the sole Arabian tree,
Who singeth only as he dies,
Sings the final ecstasy.

THRENOS

The Swan, the Dove, the Phoenix be
In no bosom, in no tree,
In no mild of memory.

Guard, nor guide no more, but slay!
Shepherd, Pastor, Teacher, lay
Staff, and crook, and book away!

The Dragon, writhing from the rocks,
And the halting, slinking, wary Fox,
And the grim, bald Vulture guard the flocks!

Love, the Son of God, is fled:
Pity, Son to Love, is sped:
Love and Pity both are dead!

Noble, Wise, and Kind are gone:
Men no more need muse upon
The Dove, the Phoenix, and the Swan!

Flowers of the Forest

FLOWERS of the forest,
Rest not here:
Winter is, and frost, and fear,
Flowers of the forest, disappear!

Trumpeter!
Give mourning call:
You have seen your captain fall,
With his back against a wall.

Defeated not!
Deserted he
By all who swore him fealty,
By love, and oath, and loyalty.

Love, and an oath!
What two are these?
They have divisions, and degrees,
Are preludes to all treacheries.

Boatswain!
Give your mates the word
—He has put away his sword—
Pipe your admiral overboard.

Theme with Variations

WHAT is love?
Tell me,
I pray!

It is eating,
Greedily,
Three times a day:

More than that
What should love give!
Eat with appetite,
And live.

.   .   .

Tell me,
What is life?
I pray!

It is sleeping,
Sleepily,
Once every day:

In that sleep
Forget, forgive,
What you eat,
Or that you live.

.   .   .

Nigh a river
Swollen by spring,
Watching growth
Of everything,
And what joy
The moon
Can bring.

Thinking
—Love
Is of the moon,
And that love
Is over soon,
And that love
Is all his boon.

Thinking
—It were better he
Were never born
Than born to be
Slave of the lamp,
The moon,
And she.

Thinking
—He had better pray
To God,
Or Woman,
As he may,
Or to the moon
That slips away.

.   .   .

In all that doth
The soul surprise
Love is wise!

Thine enemy
May conquer thee,
But not betray:

Only love
Is wise
That way:

Lover,
Clown!
Ask not why

Thy beloved
Brings thee down
To her sty?

In all that can
The soul surprise
Love is wise!

·   ·   ·

To love is all
That you may do:
To be worthy of love
All you may be:

May all that is love
Be given to you,
May something of love
Be granted to me.

·   ·   ·

I pray thee,
Tell me,
You who know
—How a wandered wight should go?

How should sing,
And to what tune?
Who of love knows not a thing:
Who knows nothing but the moon,
And the snow.

Of love, and loving,
He doth know
Not a thing:
And yet only love
Will sing:
Only sing of love,
As though
It to him
Were light
In night,
And glim,
And glow
In snow.

You—who everything do know—
Tell, how such an one should go:
How should coo,
As coos the dove?
How should sing,
And to what tune?
Who loves night,
And snow, and moon
All other things above:
And is not loved of anything,
And nothing knows of love.

. . .

All tales
Begin
—Once on a time,
Long, long ago:

All tales
Continue
—Thus it was,
And still is so:

All tell
—Of love,
And lies,
And crime:

And tell
—That love
Was crime,
And lies,

Once on a time,
Long, long ago
—Since Paradise—
And still is so.

         .   .   .

No pride hath he who sings of escape from love:
All songs of escape from love are songs of despair:
Who so hath gat him away hath got nowhere.

He sings below all that he knows as above:
He hath no mind for the gentle, heart for the fair:
No pride hath he who sings of escape from love:
All songs of escape from love are songs of despair.

Who doth not sing as the wild-dove sings to the dove,
The night-wild sprite to the moon, of love is bare:
He knows not pity, passion, praise, nor prayer:

No pride hath he who sings of escape from love:
All songs of escape from love are songs of despair:
Who so hath gat him away hath got nowhere.

         .   .   .

Let the skies,
And the seas
—All these—
And a planet or two,

With a dove,
And a fawn,
And all love,
At the dawn,

Be delivered
To you.
    ·   ·   ·

Unquestioning
—For none do question
But the enemy—
Unquestioning,
As prayer and answer be,
All that is lovely,
All that's wonderful
—The grass, a hill, a cloud,
Sunset, the sea—
Mere on a sight,
A sound,
Is ecstasy.

For all that's lovely,
All that's wonderful,
Arouses loveliness,
And wonder rouses:
And grey despair
May leap
In air:
May no more seem
In sleep

Forgetting loveliness,
In dream
Evading wonder.

.   .   .

I wish,
He said,
But what I wish
I dare not know,
And shan't explain:

Who wishes
Hath not:
And to wish
Is to have lived
In vain:

I do not
Wish
For anything;
And shall not wish
Again.

.   .   .

When to her he
Comes wooingly
—Powered by need,
Made lovely by a prayer—
And to her, waiting there,

He says
—Come,
And give,
And serve
Through all thy days:

And, all what time
We live,

I, too,
Will serve,
And give—

Every woman knows
When she doth give,
Not take,
That she doth live,
Not fake:

And knows
Her work is better than
The utmost loving
That a man,
Or that love can:

And knows
—To serve, to give
Is thine—
That only the perfume is the rose,
Only the Queen Bee is divine.

·   ·   ·

Through all thy days
To spring-time
And the moon
Give all thy love:
Love breeds its like always
—Spring-time,
And the moon,
And love —

Gentle,
Unasked,
And truthful
—Such is love—
Compassionate

Is love,
And love,
Is fruitful.

Making all song,
Making all creatures sing:
Surpassing all,
Staying
With everything:
Astonished all,
And all
Astonishing.

Spring-time,
And the moon,
And love
—The three is ecstasy—
Suspicion spies not here,
Nor near,
Nor drear
Is jealousy:
Against these is no bolt,
For them no key.

Here do all enter:
And, being entered in,
They lose all that is
Cowardice
Or sin,
And win
To trust:
To fearlessness
Do win.

She brings her timid one
To bravery:

Her knave and fool
Into her honesty:
Her brute
To friendship,
And her wise
To jollity.

Like and unlike,
When to her grace they bow,
The moon doth rise in them,
And spring allow
Green leaves
In every heart:
Laurels
In every brow.

.   .   .

Under his eave
—Where nothing may deceive—
The dove doth rest:
His love,
Her breast
Beside her love,
His breast.

Each to other is returned again:
Of love they coo,
Only of that they sing:
Now is there naught
Of two,
Or twain:
This two
Is one:
Nor is there aught,
Or anything,
That's gone.

More brave, more beautiful, and true
Than was each one
Is now this two
Who sing,
And coo:
They love each other,
And the moon,
And spring:
They do
Love everything.

.   .   .

Who saith
—I love all things,
Except the spider, and her snare—
Knows a mile of love,
And sings,
That love is here,
Or love is there:
Not, that over all she wings,
And brings
Her blessing everywhere.

Who saith
—All things I love,
Except the devil—
He is wry:
Thinking this below, above,
Somewhere, nowhere,
Never nigh:
Thinking he can woo the dove
At a distance,
On the sly.

Love is love for everything,
Fly, and spider,

Devil, God:
All that crawls
Or spreads a wing
Love doth love,
And praise, and sing:
Good, and bad,
Below, above
Beloved is,
Or love's not love.

Love is when,
Like endless air,
The sea, the stars,
The moon, the sun,
'Tis neglected everywhere,
And no one knows,
Nor doubts it none—
That nothing,
But that only love
Below,
Between is,
And above,

Love!
It is to see,
And say:
You are best
Of all, I ween:
Bravest
That has come my way:
Loveliest
That I have seen:
Kindest, wisest, noblest—Be
Noble, wise, and kind to me.

All that is, is bravest, best,
Wisest, kindest
—All is so—
There is none lovelier
Than the rest:
None lovelier
Than the ugliest:
All that is
Is loveliest:
Who will doubt
Does nothing know
Of love,
Nor shall, where'er he go.

Do you love?
Then, love are you
—No other knowledge shall avail—
To be, to know,
And so to do,
That is the truth, and all the tale:
So do, be so!
Immediately,
In each meridian and degree,
The Good, the Beautiful, the True
Is Love,
And Loving,
And is you.

In Grey Air

THIS living is a curious feat,
Is very odd!
It is to murder all we eat,
And, then, thank God
That we can murder
More than most,
Before we, too,
Give up the ghost.

It is to sleep,
And make life be
As it were not:
Dismiss to think,
To feel, to see,
And know the lot
As just a burden
And a bore,
And best forgot.

I do not understand,
Nor see
What 'tis about:
Nor why a curious
You and me
Should sleep, and eat,

And boast about
Our slaughters,
And our sleepings,
And our passings out.

.   .   .

Now that I come
Nigh to the time
When reason comes,
—Or ne'er shall come—
This I write into my rhyme

—He who talks is dumb:
He is blind who sees:
Every touching hand is numb,
And truth is not of these:
These give their idiotic own,
And by them lunacy is known.
Who sees—he sees what he shall eat,
His antelope is made of meat:
Who hears—tho' it should be a dove
Cooing in the woods of love—
Hears the grindings of his teeth,
And the growling guts beneath:
Who touches, touches with a knife,
And every touch doth take a life.

Life, taking life!
Foul mystery,
To touch,
To hear,
To see!

.   .   .

Grief arises with the sun,
And, when the golden circle's done,

Sun doth set:
But sorrow never,
Never sets,
And never rises:
Is in every heart forever,
The surprise of all surprises.

Who tells of truth,
Or beauty, he
Is a knave in his degree:
Only thirst and grief are true:
Thirst for life,
And grief for living:
Thirst and grief
Are granted you.

Put on diadem and wing
—Death and worm
Put nobly on—
Thirst shall come with you
To sing:
Grief can be depended on:
These with you are one,
And ye
Are beauty, truth, and victory.

Be contented
That you thirst:
Satisfied
That you may grieve:
Knowing
That you know the worst
Life can threaten,
Or achieve:
Die of thirst,

As all must do,
Grief shall sweeten death for you.

·   ·   ·

A moment erst,
Not seen, nor seer
—Thou art a ghost!

Say, if thou wilt
—I see,
I hear—

Make of thy love,
Or hate,
A boast:

Die,
In thy triumph,
Or thy fear,

Thou wast not,
And shalt disappear
—Thou art a ghost!

·   ·   ·

O ghost,
That has gone
Away, far away
—To another coast,
And another day:

I pray
I may
Meet with thee there
—In another clay,
In another air:

'Tis all,
O ghost,
I know of prayer
—To meet thee, somewhere,
Anywhere.

Wild Dove in Wood-Wild

NOTHING do I withhold,
And I am fair:

Do not thou,
Bold,
Adventure otherwise:

Not from me wander,
Nor me leave lone
To pine:
I am thine own,
And thou art mine.

Bereft of thee
—Lonely as lonely moon, lovely in lonely sky—
Lonely am I:

And thou,
Adventuring withouten me
—Although the buds be bursting on the bough
And the honey-combs o'erflow—
Art lonely-lost,
And hast no place to go.

Wild am I, kind am I
—As is the dove
That cherishes her dear in the wood-wild dim—
With my sweet milk
I feed my love:
And with red apples
Cherish him.

Trumpets in Woodland

THAT is a young tree growing in the wood:
This is your heart! You did not hear a sound!
Only your heart gave heed as the sap throbbed:
Only your heart!
Or only, if not that,
Yon love-grown, slender-dainty beech slip,
That lists—as listening to all that is joy,
And will all joy suck up—you heard her sing.

These are not drums throbbing in the woods,
Nor trumpets trumpeting! None rang that peal
Over the woodland!
Hearken, hark, O hark!
Above, around, within—Hark, everywhere,
The trumpet calling, the heart-lifting,
The heart-breaking! Who does not hear
. . . Again, again . . . the thunder of the drum!

Titan with Paramour

WITH what delight, with what of no-desire,
The Titan, frowning all desire away,
Hath pride of her!
He saith—She is all pearl, and lackless:
I, all stone, and nothing lack!
Afar, apart, sundered, secure, serene,
Go we, or come, come not, or go not we,
Love is between the Mountain and the Moon!

Nay, Grim! And art thou lackless? Or thy stone
Stony enough? Who yet knows love! And knows
Lack, and not-lack, and silence, and a moon!
What things are these? Or what thing anything?
See not, know not, love not!
Abstracted be!
From all that is but absence absent thee!
Thus be! For, being thus, this is to be!

That Which Wakens

Noble as sunrise, mild as even-fall:
Lucid as light, limpid as water is:
Star-like, dove-like, love-like, compassionate!
This tells what one hath seen:
This tells not her!

For beauty is not seen, beauty not told:
Not heard, not known, imagined, nor surmised.

Beauty is Goodness, Wisdom, and is God:
Beauty's own self is He: beauty is His!
And who, born of a dream,
And dreamily remembering dream,
Shall dream to that which wakens?
Or by what a dream recall
The unimaginable Otherwise
—Goodness, Wisdom, God—
Which-Such is Beauty!

Or Where Guile Find?

THERE is a nothing, is a vacancy:
There is a no, not, non, null, never, naught!

'Tis not that this is not—this is: and this
Thou art: and this the earth is: and the sun
Is this: and God, all these, is this—and can!

Who I? What may I? Or by what of guile?
Or where guile find? Or how that what apply?
Or in what problem? Or to what an end?

Not by, not round, not under, not above!
Not by a means! Nay, even, not by grace!

For, see! This all-not is! This cannot can!
Is, is its secret! Is, is its name!
Can, is its nature! Can, is what it can!
And this thou art! And can do! And dost do!

The Mighty Mother

FOR A. E.

PRESENTLY,
I am to die:
I shall die
Upon your breast:
There,
In happiness,
To lie
—In such plenitude of rest—
Every harm
Shall pass me by
In your arm,
And on your breast:
And, with but the smallest sigh,
I shall get me
Whence I came:
Shall not die to death,
Shall be
Born into it, peacefully:
Fear can only be a name
There,
Where nothing may alarm
One who sinks into his rest
On your breast,
And if your arm.

Book IX

ADDITIONAL

Midnight

AFTER SAPPHO

FAINTER and thin,
The lapsing moon has paled
From the rough sky:
The Pleiades have sailed,
Star after star,
Bending a silver mast
Into the darkness:
And the hollow vast
Of heaven clangs
Where a trumpet-wind is blown!
The hour goes, and is gone,
—I sleep alone.

Roses of Pieria

AFTER SAPPHO

BUT thou shalt die!
But thou shalt surely die!
And not again shall be
On any lip a memory of thee;
And not of thee for ever shall be said—
"She was alive!" or, "Woe that she is dead!"
Thy memory shall perish with the breath
Of thy vile carcass, and shall drop to death
As sudden as a stone falls through the sea:
Forgotten and unhonoured thou shalt be
In the deep grave for ever:
Hast thou worn
Pierian roses, or a chaplet torn
From the Muses' brow?
Thou in the gloom of Hades' house shalt flit
From pit to pit,
Watching with frightened eye
The shades that come and stare and pass thee by,
And shalt no more be mentioned, but shalt be
Lost and forgotten, dead eternally.

The Silver Car

Far on the sea, like a golden shield,
The sun hangs low:
His drowsy eye
Scarce reaches to the lonely field
Whence I am watching, but the sky
Still bears his pomp. Now red and gold,
Now glimmering pearl and grey
Blanch and are black. And now
In sober majesty the prow
Of night's dark ship westing the wold!
The trees' long shades
Melt in a whispering shadow,
And the glow, the gleam, the glimmer softly fades.

Rapt, silent, all awaits her! Lo,
Behind the clouds the Charioteer
Shakes loose his reins—the Moon swings clear!

Optimist *

I HAVE always tried to get
A better song than any yet
That has been written—and I sense,
In moments lonely and intense,
A something whirling in a blue
—But, no matter what I do,
How I keep awake, or how
I wrinkle wrinkles on my brow
And chase the flying ghost of it
With my love and hate and wit;
With every faculty of me
Exercising ceaselessly,
I but rarely get the theme
That is every poet's dream.

Late a Muse gave me to sing
Just half of just not anything:
Then I soared into my will;
I bawled upon them there until
The Nine came, horrified, and swore
They would give me all and more
If I would only stop the noise:
—But they gave me toys and toys,

Poetic stuff for little boys,
Love-stuff! Wisdom! That and This!
Enough to make a poet hiss
For very rage who wants the theme
That is every poet's dream.

I refuse to be a saint.
I have reason for complaint.
Times and times already they
Gave my poesy away:
Shakespeare got a lyric I
Could have swifted better: why
Did they send to Wordsworth such
A clutch of sonnets? Keats as much
Of odes and what-nots? And A. E.
Got a poem meant for me
—A Song of Beauty—So I fear
That, ere the mellowing of the year,
They may give away the theme
That is every poet's dream.

Envoi

Prince: I have paper and a pen!
I'm as good as other men!
Here I am, and here I sit
—Let the Muse take note of it!—
Ripe and ready for the theme
That is every poet's dream.

Vanity

A MISCHIEVOUS intent!
A pent-up goodness,
And imprisonment!
A stifled might!
Thou dost not love, nor God, nor woman, nor man:
Thou art thyself thy lover, and thy can
Is drained to thee, and to thine own delight.

But to escape? But to evade thyself?
Others so easily, although they come with steel
And roaring musket on thee—But that Elf
Within, and deep within, hath thee at heel.

Oh, tame as a fawning dog that knows no shame,
Thou fawnest on thyself, and lovest slavery!
Go, tame thy master, thou too-beastly tame!
Love nothing! Love not even God in thee,
Lest thou again be strayed away and be
But vanity!

Alas! How to forget that which is instant always!
Can self by itself be self-forgot?
Think that the sun wots not of his own rays,
Or that the aery light-paced moon be not
Instant of pearl and silver as she rides

Thrilling a world to beauty—
Be no more a self! A Thou! But, from the cell
Of isolation that makes all to swell
Important, rootless, hateful, hating still
All that will measure thee, fly from thine ill:
Thyself alone can never be thy friend:
Thyself alone can bring thine ill to end.

Be thine own enemy!
Lie thou in wait for thee!
Torment thee, and deprive thee of thy lust!
This, all alas and woe for thee, thou must
Or thou art lost, for ever and for ever, and for ever.
Thy physic this, this is thine only cure
—Take all thou art, and give it to the poor.

Like them,
Unmarked and unremembered, be
Upon no lip:
But as a ship,
All lost,
All toss'd,
All derelict and stray
Goes shudderingly,
Drifting the wild sea-way,
Rolling the bleak, waste chances of the sea;
So thou,
Go thou,
And, at the prow,
Hope terrified, hope peering if a star
Lighten thy rage and ruin from afar.

Doffing the Bonnet

INFORMED, precise, empowered, the seed
Knows present work, and future need:
Knows airlessness . . . and dreams of air!
Knows from the Dense and Dark to where
The Sun doth conjure all, and bless
Knowledge and Will with fruitfulness.

Ere she will let them from the dark,
All motherly, with shields of bark
She wraps each tendril in a skein
From the cold wind, and the cold rain,
From deadening doubt and dead delay,
From the hard stone and the harsh clay.

Deep in the dark, with rooty tongue,
She, knowing, seeks all things among;
With knowledge science never had
She knows the good, she knows the bad:
Chemist and Sage and Prophet, she,
The Finite, plans Infinity.

She springs the branch, she weights the bough,
She shapes the leaf—and she knows how
T'infuse a delicate, a sweet
—Distillation complex, neat—

340

That the quick bee, Love's Messenger,
May carry Life that's Soul of her.

   • • •

Bow a little to the seed
That knows so much, and hath no need
But soil and dew and a warm ray
From the bright smile that wakes the day
—Alone! Not lonely! Not afraid!
Bow to the Seed that the Seed made.

There Is Still a Time to Sing

THERE is still a time to sing
Before the chilly silver wing
(Silver on the under side,
Steel above) has come to hide,
Hide away and cover over
All the daisies in the clover,
All the buttercups that shake
    On the wind.

So I troll my ditty to
Autumn skies of white and blue,
Watching where the yellow trees
Drop a leaf to every breeze,
Leaves so light and wasted they
Flutter up and fly away,
Fly away until the rain
Weighs them down to earth again.

Winter hath his pallid eye
Peering whitely from the sky,
Staring from afar is he
In a cold ferocity,
And his dumb command is known
To the king upon his throne.

There is still a time to sing
Before the chilly silver wing
(Silver on the under side,
Steel above) has come to hide,
Hide away and cover over
All the wildness in the clover.

Holiday

If I could but have my way
I would go on holiday
To a place where children run
Happy-hearted in the sun:
Where there are no bounds at all
Of hedge or stream or garden wall:
No teacher, priest, or magistrate
To scowl beside a bolted gate:
Where no man could in his pocket
Stick a sunny field and lock it:
Where a draper wouldn't grin
Sickly when you ventured in:
Where a sage is never tied
To the grocer at his side:
Where a man might work as gay
As a baby at his play:
Where a thought and act would be
As a man and woman free:
—There, if I might have my way,
I would go on holiday.

Sensible People

A FIELD of corn and a bird in flight,
These give sensible folk delight.

A cat and a kitten, a cow and a calf,
These make sensible people laugh.

A dancing maid and a laughing lad,
These make sensible people glad.

The moon by night and the sun by day,
These make sensible people pray.

Shops, sermons and marriage, and dear and cheap,
These make sensible people weep.

The Rain

EVERYWHERE
The rain is falling
Through the air;
Brawling
On house and tree,
On every little place that you can see
The rain-drops go:
The roofs are wet, the walls, the ground below.

What can it be
That makes the high, wide heavens weep so bitterly?

Alas!
Trouble that does not pass:
And weariness,
And sorrow, and despair, and loneliness:
The folk who sleep
Are happy that they do not hear the heavens weep.

Midnight has chimed,
The people all are stretching, dumb and blind,
Asleep in a bed,
Save I alone who listen overhead

Unto the rain
Splashing upon the roofs and window-pane.

Midnight! and I
Can get no sleep, nor can the sky.

FOUR POEMS FROM
"HERE ARE LADIES"

I

One and One

Do you hate me, you!
Sitting quietly there,
With the burnished hair
That frames the two
Deep eyes of your face
In a smooth embrace?

And you say naught,
And I never speak;
But you rest your cheek
On your hand, a thought
Showing plain as the brow
Goes wrinkling now.

Of what do you think,
Sitting opposite me,
As you stir the tea
That you do not drink,
And frown at naught
With those brows of thought?

II

Brigid

AFTER THE IRISH

Do not marry, Breed, asthore!
That old man whose head is hoar
As the winter, but instead
Mate with some young curly-head:
He will give to you a child,
He will never leave your side,
And at morning when you wake
Kiss for kiss will give and take.

I wish that I had died, I do,
Before I gave my love to you:
Love so lasting that it will
While I live be with you still:
And for it what do I get?
Pain and trouble and regret,
The terrors of the aspen-tree
Which the wind shakes fearfully.

If this country could be seen
As it ought—then you had been
Living in a castle grand
With the ladies of the land:

The friend and foe, the Gael and Gaul,
Would be cheering, one and all,
For yourself, and, this is true,
I would be along with you.

You promised, 'twas a lie, I see,
When you said you'd come to me
At the sheep-cote; I was there,
And I whistled on the air,
And I gave our settled call—
But you were not there at all!
There was nothing anywhere
But lambs and birds and sunny air.

When it is dark you pass me by,
And when the sun is in the sky
You pass me also—night or day
You look away, you walk away!
But if you would come to me,
And say the word of courtesy,
I would close the door, and then
I'd never let you out again.

But do not marry, Breed, asthore!
That old man; his heart is hoar
As his head is: you can see
Winter gripping at his knee:
His eyes and ears are blear and dim,
How can you expect of him
To see or hear or pleasure you
Half as well as I would do?

III

Mistress Quiet-Eyes

WHILE I sit beside the window
I can hear the pigeons coo
That the air is warm and blue,
And how well the young bird flew—
Then I fold my arms and scold the heart
That thought the pigeons knew.

While I sit beside the window
I can watch the flowers grow
Till the seeds are ripe and blow
To the fruitful earth below—
Then I shut my eyes and tell my heart
The flowers cannot know.

While I sit beside the window
I am growing old and drear;
Does it matter what I hear,
What I see, or what I fear?
I can fold my hands and hush my heart
That is straining to a tear.

The earth is gay with leaf and flower,
The fruit is ripe upon the tree,

The pigeons coo in the swinging bower,
But I sit wearily
Watching a beggar-woman nurse
A baby on her knee.

IV

The Moon

If the Moon had a hand
I wonder would she
Stretch it down unto me?

If she did, I would go
To her glacier land,
To her ice-covered strand.

I would run, I would fly,
Were the cold ever so,
And be warm in the snow.

O Moon of all Light,
Sailing far, sailing high
In the infinite sky,

Do not come down to me,
Lest I shriek in affright,
Lest I die in the night
Of your chill ecstasy.

Index to Titles

Index to First Lines

358